BEGGARS
—AND OTHER—
COMEDIANS

MARTIN KARI

Copyright © 2025 Martin Kari.

All rights reserved. No part of this book may be reproduced, stored, or transmitted by any means—whether auditory, graphic, mechanical, or electronic—without written permission of both publisher and author, except in the case of brief excerpts used in critical articles and reviews. Unauthorized reproduction of any part of this work is illegal and is punishable by law.

ISBN: 978-1-63950-335-3 (sc)
ISBN: 978-1-63950-339-1 (hc)
ISBN: 978-1-63950-342-1 (e)

Because of the dynamic nature of the Internet, any web addresses or links contained in this book may have changed since publication and may no longer be valid. The views expressed in this work are solely those of the author and do not necessarily reflect the views of the publisher, and the publisher hereby disclaims any responsibility for them.

Gateway Towards Success

8063 MADISON AVE #1252
Indianapolis, IN 46227
+13176596889
www.writersapex.com

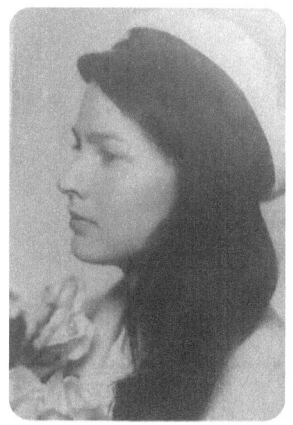 

In Loving Memory of Arja Kari

To my dearest wife, **Arja Kari**, whose journey beyond
this life has left an emptiness no words can ever fill.

Though you are no longer here to share the laughter and the
quiet moments, your love remains woven into the fabric of
my days. Your wisdom, warmth, and grace continue to guide
me, reminding me that even in absence, love is eternal.

Beggars and Other Comedians carries your memory within its pages.
For it was your spirit that taught me to look at life with compassion,
to smile at its ironies, and to embrace its trials with courage.

This book, and every word I write, is a testament to you—
a love that endures beyond time,
a presence that death cannot erase.

Cover image = Paul Gauguin, "Tahiti"
French Impressionist, 1848 Paris - 1903 Marquesa
Island of Hiva Oa (Pacific) Annotation: "Road in Paradise",
….all human beings long for the same, just varying on
their paths to get there (excerpt from chapter II)

CONTENTS

About the Author ix
Review xi
Prologue xiii

Chapter 1   Royalty 1
Chapter 2   Beggar 23
Chapter 3   Toolmaker 49
Chapter 4   Doctor 77
              1.) Family-Doctor 79
              2.) 'Pill-Pusher' 89
              3.) 'Mouth – Plumber' 93
              4.) Witch-Doctor 100
              5.) Surgeon 106
              6.) Flying Doctor 113
Chapter 5   Plumber 124
              1.) Roof-Plumbing 125
              2.) Water-Plumbing 129
              3.) Gas-Fitting 133
Chapter 6   "Comedian"—Teacher 136
              1.) Secondary Teacher 137
              2.) Kindergarten -Teacher 146
              3.) Tertiary-Teacher 153

Chapter 7	Mechanics	163
	1.) Motor Mechanic	163
	2.) Diesel-Mechanic	171
	3.) Panel Beater	177
Chapter 8	'Politician'	184
	1.) 'Honest-Broker'	184
	2.) Power-Broker	189
Chapter 9	"Garbo"	192
Chapter 10	Lawyer / 'Law-Twister'	201
	1.) Lawyer	201
	2.) 'Law-Twister'	204
	3.) 'The Old School'	207
	4.) 'The New School'	208
	5.) 'Smart-Twisters'	210
Epilogue		213

ABOUT THE AUTHOR

Born in Transylvania during World War II, Martin Kari's life followed many pathways.

Technical and then formal higher education prepared the author for a life with a sense of exploration, adventure, intellect and humanity. Having worked and lived on four continents as a global citizen, he settled in Australia with his wife and six children in 1981. It was only in retirement that he found the time to take up the pen again, proving that it is never too late to take on something new in life. Martin has published worldwide 17 books so far ranging from politics, novels, travel stories, biography, poems, children books also with own illustrations up to practical philosophy (in English and in German).

REVIEW

This is Martin Kari at his thought-provoking best! He offers, as always, some challenging ideas for us to read about and to think about. His characters come alive when we share their working and private world.

He has deliberately chosen a wide range of professions and professionals to observe and has given us an insight into their ambitions and their disappointments, be it doctors, teachers or mechanics.

Martin paints a landscape overflowing with ordinary people and then he makes them extraordinary for us, the reader. As most of our own lives are indeed "comedies", then playing the "comedian" is often our chosen role. Martin's wry sense of humour is there, if the reader but looks for it. Highly entertaining, forward-thinking and yet appreciative of life's daily dramas, this book will provide something for everyone. In the eyes of this reader, Martin's work is very readily readable as we see a little of ourselves in his clever portrayal of the complexities of 'the simple life'.

I have appreciated the opportunity to be such a very small cog in the big wheel of Martin's work. In other words, I have thoroughly enjoyed my "comedian-role".

(Joane Morish BA., University of Queensland Australia, March 2013)

PROLOGUE

The other Comedians

There is always a 'comedy' with us! Let us look closer into daily lives of a number of people in order to find out whether it is true that we all are in other words 'Comedians' and why. Here is a "mirror" for many of us to look into and find out whether or not we can recognise ourselves. To do so, we should retreat from a convenient self-understanding. With an open mind, we'll then experience that a self-recognition is all smiles here. I'm not starting where most people would consider such an exercise, namely, on the 'bottom' of our questionable 'social ladder', but rather the opposite. It is here that the 'Comedians' are overlooked conveniently. All that needs to be done, is to have an open mind, look at life in an unbiased manner and eventually behind 'Potemkin- Facades', the deceiving sights surrounding us all. How much higher can we go with our 'comedian-search' than with 'Royalty'? We won't have to look into the sky for something higher, but rather remain on firm ground. Here, each 'comedian-life' is described in a way not necessarily representing every individual. I, the author, want to play with ideas, realities and have a look into individual 'mirrors' which tell, where somebody stands in a society.

As realities are here questioned, therefore this undertaking can be called a 'comedy'. It is something to think about and compare with what we know or don't know.

CHAPTER I

ROYALTY

I let the ROYALTY go first: The early daily sunlight finds its way through the not entirely closed curtains of the tall window-centre in the Royal bedroom.

All the plush armchairs around the royal four-poster-bed, chest of drawers, mirrors, oil paintings on the walls in their carved golden frames, they all are still tinged with pale misty daylight. The silence of this splendour is broken by a sudden, cautious knock at the closed massive timber bedroom door.

"Oh, again we have to get up for another day! How I would like to stay in bed a bit longer!" murmurs the King in a sleepy voice to the Queen.

"Remember, last night was a late one, however today's duties won't wait for another day, so let's better get up", the Queen answers, clearly indicating that she is now awake.

"Today the sun is at least kind to us. It shines brightly through the curtains, where a gap has been left. Let's open the curtains first, so that our day can start well. We don't know yet, who else will be kind to us today", continues the Queen while moving out of her comfortably warm bed, sitting first upright on the bed's edge," do I have to be specially dressed already so early in the morning? What is today's programme?" continues the Queen.

"Don't spoil our day and wreck our brains. Our servant is here for that and he should know, I better call him", responds the King.- Security guards in fine uniforms open the bedroom door half way first, so that the servant can slip into the bedroom accompanied by the heavy door-squeaking. Inside the bedroom, the servant offers his 'good morning' with a deep, elegant bow.

"What is today's agenda? Please help my memory to wake up", requests the King."

"Your Majesty, if I may recall today's itinerary, there is a visit from the Earl of Dogston with his Countess at 10 am. It's about the tax, the Earl owes our Kingdom."

"Oh, this again, why is the Countess accompanying the Earl on such a mission?"

"Your Majesties, allow me to suggest, the Countess does not only bring along her good appearance, but also her very sharp mind. She is the one to be watched making decisions!"

"That is enough, look after your business, I'll let my dear Queen know, who is stealing our early morning hours."

In the adjacent bathroom, the King reminds his wife," you know what to do, when the Dogston 'bitch' turns up in less than two hours. You look mainly after her, while I tackle the Earl. In half an hour we meet in the Red-Dining-Room."

Next to the King's coffee cup, a 'Petition List' from the Royal Secretary is already waiting on the table, begging for the King's early attention. Without breakfast, the King is not in the mood to pay his undivided attention to, whom so ever is asking for it: "I do not want to see it now, leave it for later. But what I like to see today, is my Queen. You are making my day, your obvious charm will blow away the Countess. – So what have we for breakfast besides the usual standard stuff?"

"Grapes of the early harvest from down South have come on the table for your Majesty today. You will enjoy their fresh, sweet taste."

"I hope so, I'll let you know. My lap-dog is already seated. At least there is one in this damn house, who cherishes punctuality and can be trusted. What about our two children, are they up and in Nanny's care? When we've finished breakfast and if they are good children, I want them to come and see the Queen and me. I wonder how nicely they are today dressed."

"We'd like to leave your Majesty and the Queen more personal freedom this morning which could help prepare your day better ", one of the servants says.

"How would you know about today's agenda?"

"Your servants' only wish is to serve our King and Queen,"

"I'll take your word for it and we'll see latest tonight, how my day was. If the day was good, you earn my respect; otherwise don't talk nonsense any more. –Why isn't my coffee hot enough in this beautiful flower-cup? How many times do I have to say, no cold coffee for me! How long has it been on the table? Hurry up with the new hot coffee, breakfast time is almost over."

One servant then suggests: "Your Majesty, would you like the court jester to join and cheer you up?" "If we still have time for him, get him in, but before ten o'clock he has to leave."

His jester's cap in his right hand, 'Bubble Gum' as everybody knows him, conveys his morning reverence with a deep bow: "What can I see, only happy faces! No wonder the sun has decided to shine on us, too. I declare today's password that everybody is a winner."

"Ho, ho", exclaims his Majesty," my 'Bubble Gum' is keen today!"

"Just listen to the dream I had last night," continues the court jester, "in my dream I was on the local fun-fair. Everybody pushed his luck with the little money that people such as I and many others have these days. At one stall, a clown entertained a whole crowd, free of charge, while everywhere else only a few people could be seen. What is the clown's secret to win over people, I asked myself. To join this crowd, I had to sneak my way through to get closer, so that I could also hear the clown better. Aba-kakabra, our King is great, he gives back to his people what he takes away from others, soon we all will be rich."

"You better not believe it, because I can see only that you tried to make a joke. Where would the country stand with its King, when everybody is rich? Enough is enough, before you go, quickly tell me a real joke for the day."

'Bubble Gum' scratches his head as if it were difficult to crack a joke. "Well, what about this one? What do you give others and still keep yourself? – a cold!"

"You are right, keep it with you, I don't want it," replies the King. "Do you have another quick one?"

"For your Majesty, I've another one for sure. What did the lion say when it saw two hunters in a jeep? – Hooray! It's meals on wheels!"

"Hum, I like that one. Quickly another one, before time is running out!"

"What is the difference between a locomotive engineer and a school teacher?"

"Don't ask your King, you should know!"

"Well, one minds the train, and the other trains the mind."

"Now, enough is enough, we should get ready for the more serious part of the day."

While the morning party breaks up, the King and Queen retreat into their bedroom to get dressed for the upcoming reception of the Earl and his Countess. Both the King and the Queen demand that their personal servants stand in front of their wardrobes. "You make sure that we are dressed properly for the occasion. It's important, we need money!"

"Your wishes are our utmost obligation, your Majesties!"

"We don't have to listen to this any more, just do your job and I'll let you for sure know, how you've performed. And my dear Madam, don't forget the time with all your fancy make-ups. We must be in the reception in twenty minutes."

Ten o'clock a.m. sharp, everybody who is close to the King, the guards, advisor, treasurer, secretary, reception personnel, they all have gathered in the grand reception. It is all around the walls furnished with luxurious framed mirrors giving the impression simply by the mirror images that everything and everybody is bigger in size and numbers. Nobody feels here alone, but rather surrounded by glamour and probably distraction, too.

While the so important protocol is on one side for the moment running smoothly, the other side takes the liberty to arrive late. Therefore the atmosphere is tense. Nobody wants to say, what the King probably thinks: "The 'bastard' tries to pull my leg. He is not only late with his tax payments, but on top of that makes us waiting:"– The King addresses the assembly this way instead: "If our honourable guests do not turn up very shortly, I'll give them another fifteen courtesy minutes, and after that I'll call the meeting off."

Shortly after these words, a Courier announces the guests' arrival. – "When Murphy's Law still rules, how could it be different this time?"

The King pulls himself together and continues, "let's wait and see what they are up to."

"My utmost respect to our King and the Queen!"

The Earl opens his address with half a bow.

"What I can see, my dear Earl and his Countess have arrived in high spirits, which should help the purpose of today's meeting."

"Our Queen's beauty is incomparable, may I first have the privilege to kiss her Majesty's hand."

"I offer my other hand to your charming Countess and invite her to a welcoming walk into my rose-garden, so that your Lordship finds time for more pressing issues.

My dear Countess of Dogston, please feel at home, relax and follow me, a welcoming cup of tea and sweets are already waiting for us on the garden's settings."

The Earl seems to be impressed and says: "How thoughtful is our Queen! Not much else is left for us two than to look after ourselves."

The King responds: "Your Entourage is free to enjoy our hospitality under the special care of our servants. I ask security, adviser and jester to stay with us. All the best food, the country can offer, is already waiting, games and entertainment are at your disposal. You are my guests, and everybody should feel important, please make yourselves at home.

Now, what about, I invite you for a cup of tea into my leisure room? Let's first settle in after your journey so early in the day, work doesn't run away, it comes afterwards. To tackle outstanding issues, we better enjoy the early day while we can still do so. Who knows, what the day is holding for us."

In the splendid, red plush furnished leisure room, peace and quiet invite to take a seat in one of the comfortable armchairs.

"Take a seat in the one opposite to me," offers the King to the Earl, who questions without hesitation: "Is this the hot seat?"

"You are quite alert my Dear! If you start feeling uncomfortable, we can also move outside and come to the point of our meeting straight away."

"Your Majesty may well understand my comment as a joke, let's not see any harm in it."

"Joke or not, the end of this meeting will show latest in two hours our outcome. Before we are getting more serious, may I ask, how has the weather lately been in your area? "

"Even if we were to complain, it wouldn't help. Your Majesty must have good contacts to our Creator because we have brilliant sunshine on our meeting."

"I wish, I had, it's not much I can do.–Something more down to earth, how is your family and Entourage?"

"If it were only about them, your Majesty, I wouldn't know what a headache is. The public commitments, you know, are the ones that make your sleepless nights."

"Since when do I've to listen to my Earl of Dogston that he is plagued by sleepless nights? Do I have to ask your Countess about the reason, or are you referring to the tax payments you've come to present to me? I hope, neither. The country cannot afford to wait any longer for the tax to be collected so that necessary services here and out in the country can be maintained. We better retreat into my study and come straight to the point, before wasting our time for much longer. It should be only a matter of minutes, if my Earl or his Treasurer have done their homework to satisfaction."

"Talking these days is good, but when it comes to deliver, too many problems stand in the way within the country."

"I'm not here to listen to problems, can you deliver or not?"

"Of course your Majesty, I can deliver, that's why I'm here. Whether you are satisfied with my report or not, it is a different matter all together. Here are the balance papers."

"Please take a seat while I look into them."

A few long, nervous minutes pass in total silence until the King opens his address: "The sum on the bottom of your tax payment cannot be all you want to show me. Also remember, shortcomings will be deemed to your account. My position is clear, the law of the country outlines your duty of tax payments. Go back to the people and find the money they are hiding. Money is out there, you have only to clamp down on it. No excuses, I don't know why I'm always the one who has to deal with problems which I haven't caused."

"You are right, your Majesty, I'll tell my tax collector to do better his job. – On the other hand, I ask you to understand that people went through difficult times during last winter because of continuous severe cold conditions. If I may say so, the only way to compensate for this shortfall would be, to wage war and take by force the enemy's harvest-surplus."

"And who is going to pay in the first place for this operation? Don't expect me to go down this road. You go back and do your homework as expected and I'll see you latest in a month's time, but only when you deliver the money which the country needs."

"Ill try my best, your Majesty, however sugges-ting that our Treasurers put their heads together and establish what finance is available at present. This helps to take away unnecessary worries from us while we can join our ladies in your lovely established rose-garden. I wonder how they are getting along with each other. May I tell my Adjutant to call the Treasurers in order to meet here and report back to us on our return."

"Well, you've called the shots, you've also the seal of my approval. If it wasn't for money, life could be so much easier. To tell the truth, I hate this financial pressure."

"I assure you, so do I. People out there have very little or no idea of what your Majesty and 'Little Old Me' carry on our shoulders."

"Not to spoil the hour of this day, let's do what we agreed on."

At the end of an alley of endless rooms on both sides with closed doors, an exit-door leads into the open. Here a marvellous garden of clean cut green hedges with colourful flower beds in between lead straight to the adjacent rose-garden, the Queen's personal pride.

"I can see, our ladies are having a good time. May we join our two special 'roses' to give our meeting a pleasant outcome, too?"

"What are the results of your meeting? You don't look like a happy man, my Dear!" – pleads the Queen.

"Nothing to talk about now, we better enjoy the little time that is left for our meeting in your company," replies the King, continuing short after taking a seat at the beautiful white wrought-iron table-setting as the question of the time arises: "does anybody know what time of the day it is, before we get spoilt and carried away in this paradise of roses? I got the feeling, it's already around midday. Can my servant confirm this please?"

One of the royal staff keeps to the party on a closer distance and is quick to confirm the King's guess, adding the couple of minutes already passed midday. The party is caught by surprise when the Countess of Dogston claims: "We've just only arrived and the time is already running away, where is this leading to?"

She still adds however in an undertone of her concern: "Well we've no choice but to bring this matter to a successful end, so that everybody can move on from here."

"While your Treasury works on better details, we join the ladies with a cup of tea. Would my dear guests like anything else with the tea?"

The King gives hand-signals to a servant asking to bring a rich food variety from which everybody can choose to his/her liking. Then in the midst of a slowly developing conversation, the King's Secretary joins cautiously the party reminding of the day's next diplomatic visit, which is scheduled half past two in the afternoon.

Hearing this, the King asks for more details: "Who else is going to give us the honour of the next visit?"

"It's the Minister of Social Services, if I may say so."

"Aha, somehow I knew that this is going to happen! The tax collection hasn't even been finalized and here we are, the first claimant knocks already on the door. This is something for my dear Queen to look into, because she knows best how to keep this kind of requests at bay. Please remember that nothing is created from nothing! We better postpone our meeting for another time. Keep in touch, so that latest in a month's time the current tax payments can be resolved satisfactorily. My Earl of Dogston has shown at least courage in the company of his charming Countess and turned up at the Royal Palaces even with unfinished business. I give you another chance to do better next time. Please excuse me, my Dears. The Queen will partly escort you on your way back home. More urgent matters are waiting for me right now. My thanks go to you for paying us a visit."

Said and done, that was the first protocol of the day.

"What next?" – asks the King his Secretary after the party has broken up. No pomp-farewell, just a reminder to come back with a better accomplished homework. This is how far the Royal courtesy could come to the party on this occasion.

"Next, your Majesty, after lunch, until three p.m., you have the choice either to relax one hour or have a walk with your dog, see your children, or read in your study. After three p.m. the opening of the new bridge across our river is scheduled. Local representation of all walks of our community will be there waiting for you to cut the ribbon in order to bring communities from both sides of the river closer together."

"Do I have to make a speech in front of my people?"

"Like usually, your Secretary will step in and have something prepared for you in writing."

"Very thoughtful, thank you, a King has never enough time to think of everything. I only wonder if the cost of this project have gone through the roof, too. We have no choice on this matter but to celebrate first and have the surprises afterwards. People want to see the shining side of a medal. Everything else we have to keep under a carpet skilfully as long as possible, so that the King's standing cannot be questioned. I better hurry up for luncheon now, where I meet my Queen to tell her about our next protocol program. And by the way, while we are in town, Madam will like to do what all women love, shopping, spending our hard-earned money. Please remind me in time of the events we just talked about.

A good luncheon, you know, can carry us away. Anyway I'm looking forward to such a good luncheon in the company of my Queen, the Court-Jester is also welcome. Let them know, where we meet again."

In the lunch room, a written petition is placed next to the King's silverware. Just before taking his seat, the King picks the carefully folded paper which is half-way slipped under a colourful painted plate of a swan-lake scenery: "What is that paper doing here?" – asks the King the servant, who holds the solid carved wooden seat ready for the King to sit down: "I've no knowledge of it, Sire, it must be something important to be in this place." "You take it and tell me what it is, or do I have to call for my security guards?"

"Your wish shall be my highest priority!"

"I hope so, tell me what this is all about."

"The homeless of our Kingdom have raised a petition asking for your support."

"And that's it, just like that? Don't they want me to eat any more, so that they have something, too? If I answer all these people's wishes, I end up without an ordinary shirt and the country has no King any more. Hand it to my Secretary, he knows what to do with such a paper. Since when it is my fault that people have no roof over their heads? Whose fault is it? I've almost lost my appetite already. From now on no public, nor official request bypasses my administration and comes unsolicited to my attention. Do I make myself clear?"

"Yes, your Majesty, your request shall be law to us all."

"Don't talk nonsense, just do what you are told! My Court Jester receives the task now to save this lunch for me."

"I'm always ready to please my King and his Queen. Let me tell you an incident that really happened. It will cheer you up again: not our King, but one of his Dukes went for dinner into the countryside on one weekend. After a long drive, in an ordinary people's car incognito, the party arrived in a very small village of his Dukedom. They couldn't miss in its centre the beautiful pub, which caught the eye with colourful flower baskets all along the window sills. The Duke, his family, his Deputy and driver, all unanimously decided to stop there for lunch. Hardly any person could be seen in the street or near the pub, only a nearby call of geese interrupted this silence. Therefore the party managed to slip unnoticed into the pub after leaving the car parked in a spot out of everybody's sight. The people missing around this time of midday in the street were inside the pub. They had taken all their noisy chatter with them. Only for a few moments the noise calmed down until the newly arrived party had settled in one of the pub's corners with a bigger table, which could offer all of them a seat. Only after a while, the waiter made his rounds also past their table, welcoming them: "What would the lady and gentlemen like to be served? I take your orders and hope you feel at home in our pub. Today's special can be found on the separate leaflet with the menu-chart. It's the recommendation of our kitchen and can be served without much delay."

Nobody here recognised the important visitors. The menu-chart was studied rather thoroughly, before the waiter returned and took the orders. Soup was first served in a white, ordinary deep ceramic plate, of which the waiter carried two in each hand, stagged half across the other plate. The Duke watched this already from a distance, telling the waiter:

"The soup is not hot enough!" – The waiter returned to the kitchen doing what he was told and bringing along what he considers hot soup in the plates.

Again the Duke told the waiter from a distance that the soup is not hot enough. Following the guest's wish, remaining calm and polite, the waiter followed the guest's wish, returning the soup to the kitchen

Next time however, when the waiter returned the soup, and the Duke kept telling him that the soup wasn't hot, the waiter couldn't hide his surprise asking: "How does my dear guest know the soup is not hot without trying it?

The Duke was quick to answer: "As long as you carry the plates with your thumb in the soup, it certainly cannot be hot; do we agree on that?"

Red-faced and embarrassed, the waiter returns the soup to the kitchen and this time carries the hot soup with no finger in it."

"I'll watch my servant from now on, when he carries the soup. You saved my day, your story makes me hungry for a soup."

"Glad, we've our Court Jester who knows to save so many situations for us with just that extra bit of humour", adds the Queen to the beginning of the Royal luncheon.

Time hasn't meanwhile stopped, but runs short instead, before the next protocol asks for attention. And indeed, lunch hardly finished, a servant reminds the King of the time:" You are already enjoying your desert, Sire, it's time to get ready for the event in town, if I may say so."

"Who is here chasing the tail of whom? I must however admit that I still appreciate a helping hand, which reminds me in time. Let's hurry up and get dressed for the opening of the new bridge. At our arrival in the foyer, I expect everybody and everything is ready to leave, including our transport. What is the weather forecast like for the afternoon? Will the sun still be around during the opening event?

If not, my Deputy shall step in for me and I'll have a bit of my own time at least for today.

How would I like to walk in the forest, only accompanied by my dog, away from these official duties. On the other hand, I must admit, if the King didn't unite the people on such occasions, who else would do it?

My people have little or no idea about the obligations ruling a King's life. The King at the top has to show what people want to see. Fulfilling such demands every day looks like a privilege, it is however an comedian-role with all its deprivations and personal sacrifices. In reality, deprivation and sacrifices exist in everybody's life, whether King or not.

Let's move forward to another protocol-step in the name of a King's duty."

"You are right, your Majesty! The weather is on your side. It supports today's bridge-opening with continued sunshine."

"This is good to hear, let's stop talking and move into 'action gear'."

When the King arrives with his Entourage at the bridge-opening scene, the whole country appears to have come together on both sides of the river in the city centre. They all expect in awe of the King's inaugurate speech with the formal ribbon-cut. It still closes the new bridge, so that both sides of the city can meet easily and freely. Trumpets, louder than the crowd, prepare the speeches to go ahead.

The first to address the crowd is of course the King. From a platform, overlooking the bridge, the King speaks partly from a prepared speech-paper adding also his personal touch:

"We've all come together to experience this historical moment of our great city when the bridge takes away the river-boundaries. It has stopped until now people to see each other; traders, businesses, families, travellers. I can assure all of you that you will see also your King to pay a visit more often to the families across the river.

All our thanks go to the builders, who have performed this magnificent modern construction despite the difficulties imposed by the river.

Before cutting the traditional ribbon, I pass the opportunity to our Mayor to also have his say on this memorable event."

'Bla-bla, or not bla-bla, the crowd is pleased and applauds loud and freely.

A ribbon crosses the entrance on both sides of the bridge. Trumpets again call for the attention. The King stands with his Entourage on one side of the bridge, while on the opposite side, the City-Mayor is awaiting his moment to cut his ribbon-crossing with a pair of scissors. As soon as the trumpets stop, the King cuts his ribbon first and moves on to the bridge towards the other side. He is followed by security guards and selected people. When the party arrives at the other side of the bridge, the King hands his scissors to the Mayor, who proceeds cutting the ribbon on his side. Nothing can then stop people to move for the first time from one side of the city to the other after the King had disappeared from the riverside. Now is the time to celebrate in the marquees, which were specially pitched by the communities.

All this festive set up was more for the people than Royalty, because the King had to move somewhere else, according to the protocol, which says: in people crowds, security is difficult to maintain.

While the King heads back to his residence, the Queen, as planned, pays incognito a visit to the city's finest shopping facility with her personal Entourage. Specially latest fashion catches the Queen's attention. It's no surprise that the Queen almost forgets time. She keeps everybody around busy helping her to buy something new, what also the King likes. Shopping cannot last long enough even for a Queen as many women have such a habit, only with one exemption that a Queen has an almost open ended budget. Finally, time reminds also the Queen or at least her Entourage to move on with a strict daily timetable.

Once back at the Royal Residence, the day has advanced well into the late afternoon. How could the welcoming of the children be different from a Royal or no Royal? The two children are already awaiting their Queen mother: "Mama, what have you bought us from town?"

"Of course I have not forgotten my two dear little ones, but let me have first a short break with a cup of tea. You can join me in the reading room and tell me what you've done so far today. – Maid, did you hear, where I want my cup of tea? I repeat it again: in the reading room; you can bring something for the children too."

At least for the moment, peace and quiet is waiting for the Queen and her two children in the reading room.

"Mama, the teacher told us that we are going to have tomorrow our first swimming lessons. I can't wait until I can swim on my own. How long will it take?"

One question follows another while the children try on the new clothes which the Queen mother brought from the city-shopping.

Comments like: I like this or I don't like that, are constantly exchanged between the children and their mother. Suddenly a servant interrupts this harmony:

"His Majesty, the King, sends me to remind you of tonight's premiere in the theatre. Its success will go far beyond our Kingdom and therefore needs the attention of our highest social ranks. Leave the children with me. Nanny will look after them. It is urgent, His Majesty is awaiting you."

"What a circus we are in, not even one minute I can be on my own! Sometimes I wish not to be a Royal and could have more time for my family. These Royal duties take all your time, but like everything else in life, they have their ups and downs, too. Thank you for reminding me, I'll be there in a few moments."

On her way to the western wing of the Royal residence, the Secretary also comes across, asking her: "Madam, your dear sister has just arrived and wants to see you."

"Who else wants to see me? Tell her, I'm not available right now! She also could leave a message with you and organise another time. I'm so sorry!"

Before joining a social dinner with her husband and the Ambassador of the Kingdom's friendly neighbour, the Queen feels the urgent need of a shower after her visit to the city, before engaging with other official protocol-duties. For dinner, the dress has to be again different from the one for the later theatre-visit. Her Maid had already taken care of everything, so that the Queen can join dinner without further delay.

"If I had not reminded you of dinner, my dear wife, you would have got lost with your shopping, am I right? You remember the kind Ambassador of our neighbouring country. He is waiting to welcome my Queen."

"Her Majesty is again charming, even more than I can remember from my last visit. Your life is certainly running on a good keel. My respects and please allow me to kiss your beautiful hand."

"You haven't changed much and are still the same old charmer. I hope you enjoy our meeting."

"If we keep talking like this, we stay hungry in front of all this fine food," reminds the King and continues: "Let's eat first and we'll see how much time is left for a talk. Our guest is happy to join us tonight in the theatre. Until then, not much time is left."

"Thank you for looking after me as a friend. I certainly will remember it when you come to see us, also you will be more than welcome," replies the Ambassador.

Additional news from the TV let time pass quickly.

Dinner is cut short, the moment a servant reminds the King:" It's time to get ready for tonight's event. Her Majesty, the Queen, and most likely yourselves need to see your valets and lady's-maid in order to find out what outfit they suggest."

"When you say so, we better hurry up. Thank God that men have less problems with their outfits!

Nevertheless, it's us, who like to see our women fashionably dressed. Half an hour should be enough for all of us to meet again in the foyer. My dear guest, you can come with me and I show the bathroom in your suite. When ready, you are welcome to return to this room, where I can pick you up for tonight's theatre visit.

If any help is needed, my staff is at your disposal, feel yourself at home.

This Premiere, of which even I don't know much, should be a big success according to the insiders. Our presence is very much expected. I never mind to look in the theatre on the bright side of life. Life would be too serious if we had forgotten how to laugh."

Inside the theatre, the public and all celebrities give the Royal Couple a standing ovation. Not long after, the opera can take off. In the rising theatre oval, the Royals can see from their private box around to the stage. It is slightly elevated from the lowest floor. A huge purple curtain with many continuous folds runs down from the ceiling to the floor, opening and closing each performance on the stage. Personalities from public life have reserved seats in the proximity of the Royalty besides the security staff.

During the opening and especially during a break, many theatre-patrons try to attract the attention of the King and Queen. All kind of conversations are then crossing the floor freely:

"Isn't this gathering of our community a perfect demonstration of its unity at tonight's event?

I can only agree with you – our ladies again steal the show with fashion that men are virtually left in their shadows.

What a coincidence! Our ladies' outfits match so elegantly that of our Queen!

I suppose, you too attended the bridge-opening ceremony.

Isn't this a great achievement?

Shame on the ones, who didn't pay attention, unless forced circumstances prevented their participation.

Tonight's theatre performance is as good as it only can get with such a high representation.

My Lady and I enjoy this distraction from serious daily life.

I just heard the Queen to mention how she too enjoyed the orchestral part and after that, the dramatic performance of the tenor as he breathtakingly went through the difficult intonations.

Only when you have read the text, you can follow the brilliant voice

On another note, how is life treating us outside this special event?

It's everything else but brilliant. The main thing is, we still manage to keep our ground.

I suppose, if the weather had been lately a bit more pleasant, it could only have helped everybody's daily live.

We've planned already going South and catching up with the sun, which has been missing far too long.

Lucky the one, who can plan that way, while most of us have to play the waiting game in order to see the sun shine again.

Fortunately, this can be only a matter of time to see the sun again.

When it rains, we can catch up with necessary work or long overdue visits, have a rest or read and eventually attend events like the one of tonight.

The way you talk, you seem to be a real 'clever clog'. I wish, life was so easy.

With all respect, 'as you make your bed, so you must lie in it'.

You beat me again! I give up and move on from here; we shall catch up later.

Closer to the Royalty, the usual 'talk the talk', 'gossip', gets on its way, too:

"There is no question about how everybody feels tonight in such an exclusive company of so much celebrities.

I'm also pleased to meet you and your wife, my dear friends.

Something must be in the air that so many of us look happy tonight.

You must have been getting younger since we last saw each other.

In fact, I can't remember when this was.

It does appear to have been ages ago.

This evening will certainly live up to our expectations.

Be assured of the high respect, everybody has for our King and Queen.

When you say so, it must be right, because also your words are counting here.

Joking aside, how is life out in the real world?

It's tough, like usually, but we manage.

As long as we can enjoy a night like this, there is no reason to complain.

Unfinished business will look brighter on another day, too.

Now we enjoy your company and listen together to the arts." - and so forth ..., only the interval-bell and an official end can stop the patrons from continuing their chat in the theatre.

The old rule is still around, people want to see and be seen in a never ending battle of a class-conscious society. Over the years, the King and the Queen have learnt how to respectfully address everybody, namely keeping a distance with formalities.

The name of this 'game' could be called 'politics'. In reality also Royalty can trust only a few people in an open discussion. In political power games there is too much at stake for every individual, royal or not.

The ones that help lift an individual in political games on to a rank-ladder, are also the ones, who in return will not fail to knock at the door in order to safeguard their own interests. Therefore, the name of such a 'game' is to agree and promise what a majority of people want to hear and find then the excuses why shortcomings cannot be avoided. One rule however stands, not to become the scapegoat of conflicting interests in said political 'games': never shut a door, is the survival message of politics. As long as people want to look up to a higher ranking person, also Royalty is in its isolation safe from a changing society.

Royals who are these days aware of such facts and know how to constantly renew their original mandates, which lifted them to their ranks, are the ones, who still can be accepted by a majority of people.

Back to the theatre. Here a broader, but still exclusive public has gathered to receive confirmation that they can simply watch and listen to selective entertainment. In return, many cherish a hope to be seen and eventually recognised. A final round of applauses with repeated curtain calls shows this theatre event a success.

Excitement on such events is one thing, tiredness after a long day is another thing. The Queen stifles another half-yawn, trying hard to look still interested with the other theatre goers, whom she and the King know only a few by their names. The etiquette dictates that neither a Queen nor a King can show any tiredness in the public. It could take some of their image.

Much relieved, the Queen finally tells the King on their way back home in the car: "The opera was quite good, but I'm dog-tired because of the late hour! Doesn't a Queen have the right to be tired from time to time, too? It's not easy to keep up with the protocol without showing your feelings or your personal expressions. Latest in bed when asleep, everything is back to normal. Tonight I can hardly wait for it. Our guest is invited to stay in one of our guest suites tonight, because it is too late to go on a return trip."

Back in the palace, the honoured guest still shares a cup of tea in the joint reading and music room. Forgetting the late hours of the day, the King then starts a conversation on subjects others than strictly business ones.

The Queen meanwhile catches up with a few daily routines, more of a personal nature: her favourite indoor plants, have they received their daily water - are the children asleep and their room put back in order - the house cat mews for her little bowl of milk, while the Queen's favourite German Shepherd receives his bone before it is allowed to head for the night into his bedroom. This happens only on occasions like today's one, when his Master and Mistress have been out. Not much more time is left of the day. A bathroom visit is still squeezed into the last minutes of the day. The King on his part retreats as quickly as possible into the comfort of his bed, under the blanket. He ends his day with reading. The Queen on the other hand still keeps herself busy, getting ready for bed with a helping hand from one of her personal lady's-maids. When she finally can enter the bedroom, his Majesty, the King, has already fallen asleep over his book. She then turns the lights off, but not before a deep sigh:

"Oh what a day we had! Tomorrow will certainly be another one."

For a few moments she continues thinking:" Let's not worry, what tomorrow might bring. Otherwise I can't find sleep at all. Anyway the new day is only a few minutes away. It will be the same all over again that our day hasn't got enough hours to cover both, what we must and want to do."

Where the sun introduced in the morning a new day between the curtain-gaps, pale moon light farewells now the day.

ROYALTY-CONCLUSION

Not everything that shines is gold, especially in the eyes of others.

Therefore also Royalty is a touchstone in a society constantly asked to meet public expectations. This is often like a 'hide - and – seek - game', in which not to disappoint is important. In such a game Royals have in reality very little personal freedom, unless they turn their power into thumb-down-rules making them dictators.

Then again a leader has constantly to watch, who is turning against such a ruling.

The higher the rank in a society, the more commitments dictate an comedian-role. In the public for instance Royals are not supposed to violate a protocol. In a simple sense, they cannot be seen 'picking their nose' or 'farting'. Royals have to dress and appear to the liking of people, never show ill-humour and most of all, to be always right in public eyes.

To be all the time right is known however to be impossible. And here is the 'catch 22' for a Royalty, namely, to find itself in an comedian-role, too. It shows that also Royalty has aspirations like 'ordinary citizens' have. According to an established law it is said that old habits die hard, but they can also help ease life, which doesn't exclude Royalty.

In a Royal case protocol has established from early history its preferred habits. It is what Royals commonly know and therefore has become entrenched over time. They have not to worry much about not-knowing as protocol regulates answers for them. For such a reason Royalty is prevented from recognising the full extent of its comedian-role.

CHAPTER II

BEGGAR

I let the BEGGAR go second:

On which level of our 'social ladder' would a 'beggar' be and how he gets along with an 'comedian-day'?

It can easily be suggested that a new day for the beggar is likely to begin very differently from that of a previously depicted 'Royal – Comedian'.

Not a 'protocol' but still some hidden agenda rules the 'Comedian-Beggar's' daily life: "I'm not feeling hungry yet and turn better to the other side of my bed. It's too early in the day to get into any rush which in my eyes everybody seems to be in. Nothing is running away from me, I can catch up with what I need any time later. I feel sorry for the 'poor buggers' out there."

One more hour passes in the morning until a few warm sunny beams reach through an alley the window of the beggar's only bed and living room. Until then, even during summer only dim daylight is creeping through narrow cobbled streets of the surrounding long established stone houses. A worn-out table cloth inside over the window bars curious eyes from outside after dusk. As soon as sunlight lets shine miraculous patterns on the window table cloth. It's then time to stretch arms, legs and find a way out of the bed. A small, black tom-cat shares this living area.

He is not in a hurry to leave the bed-comfort. Only after his master has finished his 'cat wash' from a water jug and bowl, which always waits on a half-round table against the wall, in front of a wall mirror.

The mirror size is just enough to catch a glimpse of a face during shaving, tooth-brushing and hair combing. This doesn't necessarily happen every day, because this beggar believes that nobody is out to judge whether he is plea-sing to the eye or not. As soon as the bowl is emptied today in the back yard of the premises and the jug filled from a tap in the public lavatory. The cat then knows, it is his turn to receive his bowl of milk.

Opposite the only bed, in the corner, a small, round table also finds a place with two wooden stools. On one of them is the milk bowl for the cat. As soon as in another corner the water boils with a whistle, morning tea comes onto the table. A cigarette between two fingers of the left hand puffs away light smoke into the room, while the right hand is ready to stir sugar in the cup of tea. Cat and beggar enjoy together their first daylight. Music from a small box-radio helps drown the noise from outside. The narrow cobblestone-alley allows with a click-clack even footsteps to penetrate the beggar's window. Also increasing voices can be heard, which indicates that more people go after their daily business. This is now an invitation for the beggar to move outside and start the day in earnest. From then on he watches what people leave in his basket.

Only another sunset will steer beggar-steps back into a silent solitude. An outfit is usually no concern for the beggar. Very little will also do. Depending on the weather, a decision is made what of that little clothing goes with the beggar. He too has his pride when he puts either something different or more of the little on he has got. Why is it 'his pride' and not 'her pride'? It is interesting that men are drawn more often towards begging than the opposite sex. Probably at a later point this will find its own explanation. There is no rush when it comes to a beggar's concern.

A cold, stiff breeze makes the beggar pull down only more the brim of his hat. He knows too well from a beggar-colleague, who has no luck when it rains. Buckets are placed permanently in his room to catch the plink-plonk from the ceiling. Balmy, sunny days are always on the other hand every beggar's delight, too.

Today is again one of these fine days, which is already reason enough to be just a happy beggar. Off finally he goes when the wall-clock rings ten times in the morning. He leaves the cat behind in the bed's comfort.

As soon as the only door to the room closes behind him, just a few more steps separate the beggar from a pulsing life on a public road.

A look to the right and left from the side-walk of the house-door-steps saves the beggar from running into busy-bodies who are already around during these advanced morning hours. Nobody takes particular notice of somebody else, everybody seems preoccupied in a general rush. It prevents him/her from looking around more to see even a beggar. This doesn't however worry the beggar, who is used to be overlooked.

To attract the attention of the public, a beggar needs to look different from a main stream. Only judging an outer appearance from top to toe would not help much a daily struggle at the end of such a road. What else is required to live a life not on eye-level with a society but on the edge, is a beggar's secret recipe. Does this humiliate a beggar? If he is a real beggar, not at all. Real begging stands for independence as one wants to see it, no matter what the cost.

Our beggar now moves on with the street-people barely noticed closer to a central place in town, a shopping mall, train station or sometimes for a change also a hospital. From sheer habit, the shopping mall has become his most frequently visited place.

No wonder, because people visiting shops, usually carry money of which a beggar likes to see a part going also his way, no matter how small those alms might be. 'Many a mickle makes a muckle' likewise every little bit helps a beggar, too. After barely a walk of ten minutes, not exactly at the entrance of a shop, but rather in a respectful distance a house wall invites him to stop and sit down on the pavement. However not before a cushion from under his arm goes first onto the ground, which allows him to sit down in relative comfort with his back against the wall.

The long trousers follow stiffly the knee-bend on the ground. Only every now and then the trousers end up in a bucket of water for cleaning. This is not a beggar's worry, if asked, he would eventually say only this: so far not many have died from washing not enough. The same applies for shoes. They last and last, remaining loyal to its owner until a toe sees fresh air or the sole cannot keep the foot clear off the ground any more.

A jacket holds the only colour of our beggar's outfit. Its deep pockets on the sides can hold much of a day's 'donations', his pride. Latest here, I should give the beggar of my story a name, Jim.

When it doesn't rain, on the head the wide brimmed hat is not needed. The hat then joins Jim on the ground in front of his crossed legs. Another pride for Jim is his long, wavy hair tied with a band orderly behind his head. To complete the picture, a pair of sunglasses make up the final touch for Jim. He remembers, when years ago things were still running smoothly, a family member went to the expenses buying him this pair of sunglasses in his company. It was his fortieth birthday, which he will always remember.

These days, Jim is content with the fact that a beggar's life is made of innumerable little and not big things. To battle 'big', belongs to the rich. It also took him quite some time to get through to this insight.

One of Jim's secret is to do efforts as little as possible, which in his experience doesn't only save him wear and tear of the little things he owns, but also saves him from buying more food than is absolutely necessary.

Isn't life also about making habits of something? Habits certainly differ like a 'box on an ear'. Jim takes his time and observes other people while thinking about it.

Once his hat is placed with a few coins from previous collections in front of him on the ground, a daily routine has started for Jim. It should help invite other coins to join more freely while watching and eventually being watched. It can happen in between that the dull ringing of a coin from a pedestrian in his hat startles Jim out of a dream into reality.

Sometimes the coin-ringing is accompanied by a few words from a by-passer; no coin and words only; most of the time however no coin, no word:

1. public-comment: 'you must be suffering from deprivation'
    beggar-response, tacitly: 'better watch yourself'

2. public-comment: 'here is something for you to cheer you up on this beautiful day'.
    beggar-response: 'one friendly person more in this world'.
    tacitly: what a difference friendly people can make, I bet the man is in his thirties according to the coin tossed from high up with a distinct noise' - 'thank you very much' also follows.

3. public-comment: 'as you make your bed, you must lie on it'.
    beggar-response: tacitly: 'another know-it-all-better'.

4. public-comment: 'every little bit helps' beggar-response: 'you are an angel, God bless you'.
    tacitly: it could only be a woman over forty, who bends down and hands a coin into the hat almost silently.

5. public-comment: 'when you work, you have not to be here'.
    beggar-response: tacitly: do what you like, but leave me alone.

6. public-comment: 'move away from my shop window, my customers are otherwise embarrassed and don't want to see me'.
    beggar-response: tacitly: what sort of people have the upper hand today?
    What is this money-pusher up to?

'I do what you ask me to do, straight away; I don't want to harm anybody, you are the boss'.

7. public-comment: 'you are here again today; this time around I'll let you have the left-overs from my shopping, times are getting tougher'.
beggar-response: 'we can't win any more, the poor get poorer while the rich get richer; fortunately some good people are still amongst us; you have a pleasant day, too'.
tacitly: what person this might be? a public servant, an educated person, a worker, probably a teacher, the way the coin went into my hat suggests a higher ranking public figure with a bent for religion.

8. public-comment: 'While turning his attention to other pedestrians: get out of my way, I can't afford to throw money away; and where would the world end up, if everybody begs for a living'.
beggar-response: tacitly: I've nothing to say; I thought we are all free to choose our way of life, who has got a problem here? Not me.

9. public-comment: You are still hanging around here.
beggar-response: tacitly: typical busy-body, time for nothing, not even for one word, but his donation is also appreciated.

10. public-comment: 'I wish, I had your time; money cannot buy you time; we can't have both, time and money; here is my little money for you; I wish it could buy me more time'.
beggar-response: tacitly: Vow! This is like a jackpot to receive for a change a note instead of a coin. Is this lady sure about giving away a whole day's toil of a beggar?

'You made my day, thank you, I'll remember you. Have a nice day, too'.

One main difference between town-people and Jim is that a beggar has more time to watch. From this experience he gains a necessary beggar-confidence to have collected at the end of a day enough money in his hat, so that also he can live in a relative comfort. Jim is used to controversies fellow citizens bring up when they turn away in a circle in front of him. People then seem to be embarrassed because they don't know what to do with a situation different from their own. Some people are the exemption when they connect at least with a few words to Jim.

Even from silent by-passers whole stories are unfold here in a beggar's eyes. Speaking is silver, silence gold also for Jim. In silence he is as free as any beggar can be, thinking about everything what his head can take.

The 'comedian' has learnt by now when to see, listen or speak and when not. Therefore it is easy for Jim to only observe people and not get involved in anything.

This distance has so far saved him his personal freedom. Not all people are friendly what even the eye cannot tell. Thoughts can work instead freely in Jim's head: "Where is everybody heading today and why? What is all this rush about? If all people were rushing in front of me, probably none of them could become aware of me. I seem to be lucky when somebody out of this crowd slows down and finds a penny to put into the hat in front of me. When the waiting makes me half-asleep, no doubt even then I find quickly words to thank the person who put money into my hat. This doesn't happen often, but when it does, I feel so good and forget at least for moments that I'm in the eyes of so many people the 'poor bugger' or 'beggar' they conveniently call me.

Isn't it amazing, what a few words can do, transforming a beggar's isolated life, even for moments only, into a shared life with others. On the other hand, people who cannot talk or want to talk must be so busy with themselves that they obviously lack time. Aren't they the real 'poor buggers', because they are not aware of it? Whereas I can live with it. Time allows me to ignore what I don't like."

In the midst of being lost in these thoughts, Jim receives a wakeup call from his stomach that it is time to pay attention also to it. A look into his hat-coin-collection tells him when he can have a break to calm his stomach-rumbling. In case not enough money has found its way into his hat during the day, Jim also keeps in his deep jacket pockets some change from previous days. He knows too well that every day is a different one, depending on many facts, which also a beggar cannot control: weather, people's mood, authorities having their say which sometimes forces Jim to move somewhere else. - "I rather stay on the safe side with my life style and keep some 'bobs' aside for less successful days," which is not the only insight a beggar should bring 'on board his very own 'ship'.

At the market, only a few minutes walk from his location, Jim buys a variety of food direct from small producers, who also struggle to make ends meet. Prices are here more for a beggar's budget: one carrot, one tomato, one onion, some bread-rolls, a small container of milk, a little cheese. All this will do to carry Jim through the rest of the afternoon.

On nice days, Jim heads for a bench within the town's green area, takes a seat. He is often able to claim the whole bench for himself. Today is the exemption. A man and a woman, probably in their fifties, both dressed fairly civilized, occupy already the bench. Jim hesitates to take a seat and before he walks away, the man openly invites Jim to share the bench:

"You don't mind?" Jim almost stutters. An unexpected conversation unfolds, keeping both, Jim and the couple an hour or so, longer than they could anticipate, engaged in telling each other's life story, much longer than they ever thought. "You don't work, what are you both doing in town in the middle of the week?" Asks Jim while sitting down. The gentleman next to him introduces his wife and says:

"Well, I don't have to ask you this question, we come every Wednesday into town to do the shopping which we can't do in the small place where we live. Most of the time when we go to the shopping centre across the road, we also see you. How is your day going so far?" - "I can't complain, every day is a new one for me and I take it as it comes. Talking and having a lunch break doesn't go together well. May I have my lunch while we share this bench. Will it disturb you?"

"Not at all, do as it pleases you. I'm still curious about what you call lunch."

"Nothing special, just simple food which keeps me healthy inside. My little rucksack keeps everything what I need; a plate, a cup, a set of cutlery, all wrapped into a towel, made ready to take my shopping from the open market across the road. I like your company, because it rarely happens that somebody wants to stay with me and engage in a conversation. I take my time and because you are not in a hurry, may I suggest that you talk first while I have my lunch. As soon as I've finished, it's my turn. This way we make the most of our conversation."

"My compliment, you are well organised! We both, Ann and I, are more than happy to share our time with you, so that we hear first-hand about a life of, how would you call yourself?" - "A citizen of this town, will do for the moment. If you like, I can tell you more when it is my turn." – "At a first glance, you don't seem to be the ordinary beggar, people commonly like to call somebody, who they can't fit into their blinkers-vision. We try not to belong to these people, because we think we've seen enough to know that there is usually more behind something or somebody, than the eye can see. – My name by the way is simple and straight forward, John. As I mentioned already, on Wednesday once a week, Ann and I take the bus from where we live, Newstead, to the city. Wednesday is our day off from school. During the other days of the week we try to lift the education level of our younger generation. As teachers, we face today from all sides obstacles: the government wants this, parents want that, students bring their own ideas into the 'education game' and above all, missing discipline often makes a teacher's task unnecessary difficult. People have little or no idea what today's 'education-circus' is all about. There is not much you can do, when you work for the government. In the end, we all are in one and the same boat; spending the money, is the easy part; keeping it together is something else. I don't think, I've to tell you about it. Still it is nice to buy something you like and therefore we like to come to the city. The city has more shopping-bargains. Today we look for some clothes for the arrival of our winter. It's a never ending circle. After money spent only more wishes are born. I'd like to hear what you have to say about money, which is never enough. Otherwise also our days are pretty ordinary, work, again work, to find some sleep and occasionally have a break from all this. Our two kids, George and Katherine, manage their lives more or less on their own, giving us now some hard earned personal freedom. You probably know well enough, what it means to raise children these days, don't you?"

"I'm listening. My lunch break is over. Let me store everything properly back into my backpack before I talk, if you still want to listen, what an 'old bugger' like me has to say.- Now I'm ready. It's nice to meet you on such an improvised occasion. My name is Jim, former professor at the University of Tobalu." – "I'm sorry to interrupt you, what did I say before that the eye can see never everything. This however leaves me short of words; did you say, you were a professor at a university? And which faculty, if I may ask? I can't believe that we have the honour to talk to a professor!"

"Take it easy, don't rush things unnecessary. That was back many years ago, when also I climbed the success-ladder. Only finding out, Once I'd been up on that ladder, I found out, there were only two options: option one, struggle not to fall off; option two, come down again, because life up on top is lonely and there is nowhere else to go. Science can become a path in the dark.

To bring light into it, is not only hard work but questionable, too. When I asked myself, whether this is really what I want my life to be, it was already too late to save my family from falling apart. I thought, my wife, also an academic, could help understand each other in the professional field. It turned out not to be. I never claimed to be a genius, but I do question whether it is fair that my wife took out of the blue off with a fellow from Tanzania, leaving me 'high and dry'. I found myself no doubt in the dark. The fate of my two kids is too distressing to even touch this subject any further. – Do you really want to keep listening to a fallen climber as he struggles to come to terms with his life? It's true that life goes on anyway, though conditions won't stop changing. "

"Speaking not only on my behalf, I know my wife shares this view of not putting our noses into other people's business, don't you Ann? On the other hand we also know how helpful it can be to have somebody to talk to. Feel free to talk to us, we understand."

"Lucky you, to have a wife by your side. Here I am, ousted like a leprous. But it's still not all bad. As long as we live, we don't stop learning. And I've learned my lessons. That's why I'm today here with you. From the outside I've changed, inside I'm still the same, trying to climb again this devilish ladder in order to comprehend what went so wrong in my life. What else can we do? If we could forget the past, would that give us a new, better start? But how could we possibly disconnect us from our past, which at the time appeared to mean so much not only to me.

A family cannot be excluded here. Time has become the best healer also for me. I'm not worrying any more about tomorrow. Come what may. Since I own that little I've got today, most of my worries have gone.

Isn't it greed and money that divert us from real life-issues? The more we have, the more we want. It seems like a never ending cycle. Today however, the sun shines for all of us and this is what matters.

Everything we do, is receiving this gift of a sunshine. I think, I spoke enough and don't want to waste more of your time. In hindsight, I could ask myself also: how come that I sit here in your company and talk? It has become a rare event in my daily life that somebody takes time to engage into a conversation with me. Not only bad, but also good things catch up with us without appointment. Today is my lucky day and I thank you so much for your understanding and company. I feel as if a lump in my throat has gone of a sudden, talking to somebody freely again. You don't hold this against me?"

"Not at all! On the contrary! May we suggest to meet also in the future in order to deepen our conversation. You have lost now some valuable time for your donations. We are not standing in your way and are more than happy to compensate you with our donation. You also have to promise that we can pick you up, probably on Sunday and invite you into our home."

"If you mean what you say, it's too good an offer to refuse. Do you really want to leave this note with me? This is more than I can expect during an entire day."

"Go and buy yourself something nice to remember us. We all live also from something else than bread alone. I did the talking this time, while Ann was listening. Another time, I'm sure, we'll talk about the good things that happen to us and Ann will have her say too. Take care of yourself, be happy. Where and when do you want us to meet you this Sunday?"

"I've first to think whether I can accept your kind offer. This didn't happen since I retreated from daily pressures. Please don't get me wrong, I'm lost for words for quite sometime by now. Can we postpone this meeting another week which gives me more time to prepare myself, so that you are not disappointed. We too shouldn't rush things like everybody else does. Let's rather take our time to give anticipated joy also a chance. On that following Sunday, what time would suit you to meet at the shopping centre entrance?"

"I'm sure you'll lose your concerns the more we shall have an opportunity to reconnect you with the world that seems to have gone missing for you. You still got life in front of you and can make something good out of it again. It's never too late to make a new start. You have more than enough intellect to support you in a new move. As you already said, not everything is only bad, depending on which side of the equation, bad or good, we focus and try to ignore the other side.

Returning to the time of our meeting, we suggest lunch time, twelve o'clock. Will that suit you?"

"Anything good of this nature, will suit me. One thing however I'd like you to accept that this is me and I'm not changing in a hurry from a life that has given me personal freedom back. I rather remain the 'comedian' in the eyes of other people than to relinquish my freedom to the expectations of others. Having said this, I'm looking forward to meeting both of you again. You are extraordinary good people."

"I acknowledge your determination and respect you. We'll see what the future holds in store also for you. Ann certainly wants something to say to you, too, before we go back where we need to go."

"To meet you Jim, was a lucky coincidence. We live too much isolated in our own world, hardly recognising the many different worlds other people live in. You opened our eyes more to what really goes on in our community.

I never really thought that it is so easy to communicate with people, who we wrongly consider to be on the wrong side of the society. We all have in common aspirations, a longing for personal freedom, right for work, free expression and so forth. All this differs of course from individual to individual and I learnt for the first time what somebody has to say who is a so called 'silent citizen'. Nobody's voice should remain unheard. Encouragement not becoming disconnected from society's mainstream, could save many people, who live on the edge of a society. Let's try to get a better under-standing of each other, in particular, how our surprising meeting with an inconspicuous professor is going to continue. I too reach out to you with my hand inviting you to be our guest on Sunday a fortnight. Take care of yourself. If you need to contact us, here is our home-phone number. Feel free to give us a call."

As they part, Jim doesn't take the direction back to the shopping centre. His footsteps hasten him to head home earlier for a change. The grocery shop on the way receives a rare visit from Jim today. The shop owner recognises the rare visitor and cannot but ask: "have you got money to pay me?" – Jim has only a flash of a smile on his face, ignoring this special welcome. Today he selects a chicken straight from the grill, French fries, one avocado, broccoli, one garlic and to round it off, one bottle of white local wine. This saves Jim cooking something for the day. Before facing the shop owner at the check-out, the cat is not forgotten, cat-food tin of fish joins Jim's basket. "You must have your lucky day to pay for all that. Where did you find the money? "Jim keeps quiet, thinking by himself: this is none of your business, don't stick your nose into other people's business. – From the change Jim receives into his hand, he works quickly out that alone this will get him comfortably over the next two days without having to touch his small money-reserve.

At home, the cat immediately realises that something special must have happened. His Master turns up earlier than usual. The size of Jim's rucksack reveals to the cat, something must be also in for him. Still on the bed, he arches its back before jumping on to the ground. Where Jim places his rucksack, the cat rubs at Jim's legs forwards, backwards and around with high expectation. Out of the rucksack first comes the fish-tin, welcomed by repeated jumps of cat-joyfulness into the air. He tries to catch the goodies with one paw higher up. Only after the cat has received on the floor, under the window his day's bonus in his bowl, Jim can prepare his 'banquet' on the table.

The afternoon sun still reaches through the window corner the modest one room accommodation. Noise from the road has already started diminishing, giving room to an atmosphere, pleasant for Jim.

While tasting his 'banquet', the day's events pass again in front of his eyes: "does this friendly couple really know, what a beggar's life is like and that beggars are not all the same? I've willingly chosen this life and found my personal freedom; of course at a prize, knowing also that nothing goes in life without a price-tag. There is however a majority of 'drop-outs', 'transit-actors', failures or simply call it comedians, everybody is free to name it as it suits him/her. As a matter of fact, I now can look forward to meeting new people again from the other side of the society, people also convinced that they are right with their choice of life. I'd like to find out, who out of our trio, John/Ann/Jim, has got the better convincing-power. We all have seen that not everything that shines, is gold. I'm happy, particularly today. Let's take one step at the time. The smaller the step, the less likely I'm going to slip. Any hurry won't help here either.

The coming days, I'll think thoroughly how I can meet my hosts on the same 'eye-level'. I'll be the guest and my head tells me that a good guest has obligations, too. I better don't wreck my brain too early, there are still enough days ahead to settle this issue.'

The rest of the beggar Jim's day remains on an even keel, which means, resting, reading and listen to the radio. And when the darkness of the night has advanced enough, Jim joins the cat on the bed. Purring of the cat carries them both into their dream world. Jim doesn't visit pubs, because he knows too well from other beggars where this can lead to: no money left in a beggar's pockets. Another day will then be only more of a struggle to win back what has been lost only hours earlier.

Smoking too is not an issue for Jim. Adding alcohol and cigarettes to a beggar's shopping-list, won't help the beggar's budget at all. Therefore Jim reassures himself: why wreck myself with something, which I can avoid in the first place. To come to such a conclusion, wasn't all that easy even for Jim. He is adamant that all human beings long for the same, just varying on their paths to get there.

Jim's next days continue as usual with the exemption of his growing anticipation for the coming Sunday. He doesn't want the idea to keep him awake during the night, so he decides to go next morning and see the local formal-hire-shop. An elegant suit is what Jim has on his mind. Only dressed appropriately, he feels to have the confidence to answer such a surprising invitation. And indeed, also the hire company cooperates, accepting a special deal, but not before Jim has gone to great lengths and explained the circumstances. The gentleman actually knew the teacher-couple and wanted to give a helping hand, too. A 'bob' more or less in his business wouldn't change much. Satisfaction of being part of a plan for a good purpose, was worth more in his opinion. Not only bad, but also good news spread freely, helping a business in the end, too.

Time before that Sunday flies. When it arrives,even the sun shines as if ordered. Jim already waits in front of the shopping centre well ahead of the agreed lunchtime. No one would recognize Jim today in his almost made to measure bluish suit. The wine-red bowtie only emphasizes Jim's readiness to give a good impression.

And indeed, so good is the impression that the teacher-couple cannot first recognize Jim, the beggar, from the ten days earlier. Jim makes himself noticeable by waving one hand towards the repeatedly slow passing car of John and Ann. The red, nice looking car then stops in front of Jim. Down goes the door window. Not two, but four eyes try to figure out who the person is behind that waving hand. "Ann can you believe that this is Jim we met the other day? I better get out of the car and have a closer look. - It is Jim, all right! What a surprise! Ann we are going to meet a global gentleman!" - Ann couldn't stay back in her car seat. She too got out of the car. Only a few steps away from this gentleman, she recognized Jim's face. "What is Jim doing? Hiding behind a noble façade? You are welcome, noble or not. Please join us in our car."

In the car, Jim breaks his silence: "When you go through so much efforts and pay your attention to a poor bugger, or call it beggar, I want at least show my appreciation to mark the occasion also with my efforts.

Thank you for picking me up and not forgetting about what was said when we first met ten days ago. To say something is one thing, but doing it, is often something else. We all experience this, whether a beggar or king. The only difference is that a beggar can more appreciate when words and action come together. A beggar has learnt not to expect much from fellow citizens. It turns out so much nicer when people like you stick to what they've said. While waiting in front of the shopping centre, I couldn't help thinking whether or not I'll make a mockery of myself in case you people won't turn up. This wasn't the case, I've got therefore a double reason to be happy. – You too look happy today. No wonder, when you can drive such a beautiful car."

"It's not the car, Ann and I are so happy to find you in good spirits. No doubt, we'll have a nice time together. You don't mind we have music on the radio while driving?" – "As long as it is real music and not this modern stuff, which I'd rather call noise. I should also not forget to kindly remind you that my tomcat wants me back by seven o'clock tonight. He would be otherwise very upset. – Can you hear me from the back of the car, or we better continue talking after our drive?" – "We can hear you and like to listen to everything you say. Time for a talk has always been valuable."

"It feels as if I wanted to escape from my 'comedian-role'. All of a sudden there are people in my life, who also listen and do not pretend knowing everything better like so many people do out of personal insecurity.

Hasn't knowledge become at least partly responsible for the division in our society? Only fighting brings us with time again down where we belong to. I'm speaking here out of my own experience. Methods of fighting each other vary of course mainly according to an education level.

In the end it's all unnecessary fighting."

"While talking, time has brought us quicker to our destination, Ann's and my home. Jim and Ann, please get out of the car before I enter the garage.

This way you can open your door more comfortably. –Well this is it, Jim, today you are our guest, you are welcome."

"I can see, you certainly like your garden. The care it receives from you, it responses with beauty. Isn't everything that is natural also beautiful?"

"How right you are, we can look around the garden while Ann puts the kettle on for coffee, tea or whatever you are used to."

"For me, tea please. Where I live, I don't see flowers. That's probably why I have a special liking for them. Look how your roses, azaleas over there, camellia on the corner of the house, our native grevillea and bottle brushes, they all look at us with shining colours.

Everybody who looks at your garden feels happy, not jealous, because your garden is here for everybody to look at. We don't have to own everything to be happy. When we can share, then happiness reaches out to others, too."

"Let's go into the house, women don't like calling more than once, when ready with their cooking. Watch your step in front of the house door. If you don't mind, leave your shoes at the entrance. Slippers are ready to put on instead." – "Where did you pick this custom? To my knowledge, this is for instance common in Japan. It's a compliment to the housewife not to spoil her housework." – "You are dead right. A couple of years ago when Ann and I visited Japan, we found this custom very practical. Since returning home from that trip, we changed over to this Japanese custom. We are lacking in general much in exchanging practical cultures, because old habits knowingly die hard." – "I'm pleased to listen what you are saying. During my time at the university, I came in contact with people from different nationalities. People from Asia I experienced to be very adaptable, including the young ones.. Their customs become evident to the good observer often only in a repeated closer contact. It can happen that they hold back another language out of respect for the other side, not to violate their feelings by using their language not good enough. This doesn't however mean, they are not understanding. There is a fine line in an understanding which when not treated with caution, can easily lead to misunderstandings."

"When we keep talking here in the entrance hall, we'll stay hungry so close to the delicacies Ann has prepared on the table. Let's move into the living room first and if you wish, I show you around our house.

The house was built, we'd say today, in the old, good days. Then, no materials were saved, that's why even after decades the house is still in an excellent condition. It will outlast us and look into a far future.

As I said already, our children, George and Katherine, are grown up now and have started leading their own lives. I'm confident that this will be not our only coming together. Another time, George and Katherine will be with us to get to know you, too. You see, here are still their two rooms, which they usually leave as they like. The only difference is that in their absence Ann keeps also these rooms clean and tidy. After the bathroom comes our bedroom. A spare room is considered for guests.

And now we are in the dining room, which is connected with the living room. So much for a welcome and intro- introduction. – Ann, we are also here now, when can you join us?" – "Take a seat, lunch is on its way."

"Your home is like that of a king. You must be proud of it. A lot of work must be going into such a big home to keep it so nice and clean. My compliments, the single room in town I call home is enough for me to look after. Who of you, I suppose your wife Ann, earns the respect doing so much work maintaining your family home?"

"I can now join in a conversation, too. Lunch is on the table. We like healthy cooking, a little bit of every-thing, so that Jim can easily choose what he likes. We are happy to have you with us and do our best that you can enjoy our get-together. Let's not forget eating because of talking. There is enough time afterwards. We join our hands and thank the Lord for His generosity. You know well enough Jim, we never ought to take a good life for granted. Too many people in this world are deprived of it".

"People aside, my contribution to this excellent looking hot main dish is a candle-holder I carved out of a lime-wood which is part of my meagre possessions in my town-accommodation. Time is not an issue any more for me. I've plenty of it available to choose what I like best to do in my leisure time. The light of the red candle can only add to this magnificent atmosphere. It shines on all our faces the colour of love. I hope you like it."

"Very thoughtful! I can assure you that we know to appreciate your kind gesture. We are now ready to taste Ann's magic art of cooking. Help yourself, because we can't know what you like to eat.

There is plenty food available, don't hold back. You probably remember the saying, too: A full stomach doesn't like to study. After this lunch, we won't study, but rather sit down in the living room and continue with our interesting conversation. You also don't need TV to be entertained. People today lose more and more skills to communicate with each other. I call this an art. All these modern techno-gadgets: videos, mobile-phones, TV, games, make it too easy for everybody not to do much anymore. It's today no joke that people talk to each other via the mobile-phone, even in close proximity like sitting around a table.

Don't worry, we leave our mobile phones where they belong to: business and emergencies. There is no harm using a mobile-phone, but we should not let it take over our personal communication skills."

"This is no problem for me! I've never even thought about a mobile-phone.

Not only because of where the money should come from, but also, why should I satisfy marketing strategies of the big players in our societies?" – "In a sense, you are not wrong. When it comes to control people-masses, the individual has little choice to either follow like sheep or get stamped an outsider. A 'beggar' finds himself here in the company of outsiders."

"Who is here the 'comedian'? The 'follower' or the declared 'outsider'? I'm strongly suggesting that one or another way, we are all 'comedians', differing only as to how conscious we are."

"Here, the professor comes in, who uses his brain more than the average person. I can't remember having lately with somebody such a refreshing conversation. Nevertheless, lunch is coming to an end and again, we both, Ann and I hope you enjoy our company."

"It's true that also I cant remember having spoken so much during an afternoon. Much can remain hidden only over a period of time, concerns, happiness, anger, hope. And when the moments are right, all this can come out like a blocked 'torrent'. Important for me is and was that after a 'torrent' whatsoever, the personal freedom can return.

I'd like now to propose a toast first to Ann for her culinary skills, thanks and cheers! Then a second toast goes to the couple of this magnificent home: may your care for others give you in return the personal freedom we all long for.

Over a glass of your good wine, the outlook on life shines brighter again."

"You hit the nail on the head, only confirming that a shared joy is double a joy! How about, we move on from here until Ann does the dishes? Let's sit down comfortably in the living room and please take your wine-glass with you. Do you like any games?"

"Games are not my strong side, life is already enough a game. The only game which makes sense for me, is to play chess."

"Do you like us to have our first round of chess? Let's bring it on and enjoy it together. We can still continue with our conversation, or are you such a serious player that you don't want to be diverted from the game?"

"To be honest, I'd like to do one thing at a time rather well than try to do too many things poorly at the same time."

"The professor seems still to be with you more than the comedian-role of a beggar. It will be interesting to see, how we are getting along in a game. Games often bring out people's emotions. I let you go first and choose out of my closed hands the starting set: Well luck is already on your side, you got the start! – Are you a chess-expert by the way? Your first moves give me already some headache."

"I don't want you to have any headache. It is my great pleasure to have your company. Let's not forget, this is only a game! Sorry, so soon to tell you: a check-mate!"

"Vow! This is not the beggar, this is a professor! Where have you got these skills from? Not from the street! Ann come quickly and have a look, here is a chess-champion. - One more game, which Ann also should watch. This time, it's my turn to start the game and you let me choose from your closed hands the next starting set. Well, black hopefully won't mean that I'm from the start 'in the black' again.

Here is my first move and from now on I too better concentrate on my moves."

Ann also watches the game, biting her lips in order not to interfere in the game. It takes only marginally longer until John again faces a 'check-mate'.

"We've to play more often to learn from you, Jim. How often do you play?"

"Before time turns too boring for me, whether on the road or in my own home, I pull out my miniature chessboard and start playing against myself. It's amazing how a game goes, when you've to think for and against yourself. 'Beggars can't be choosers' and 'necessity has always been the mother of inventions'. I really never feel any boredom."

"You've beaten me, in the best sense of the word. The beggar from the town's shopping centre has shown Ann and me, the two teachers, how its done, just like that.

What other talents do you carry secretly with you? We are used to keep certificates for everything we can do. Speaking on behalf of me, I feel I got the short end of the stick."

"I don't want to hurt none of you, you are so kind to me. How can I make up for it?"

"Don't get me wrong, I'm only trying to get over something which I cannot completely understand: There are people who can surprise, because most of us know very little about each other. Our secret social barriers are here in the way. – Ann, put the kettle on for one of your nice coffee. For Jim get a cup of tea ready, please.

Jim, you can stay also for tonight's dinner. We'll take you back home again in our car. You are also welcome in the future. This is hopefully going to be the beginning of an extraordinary, good friendship."

"Slowly but surely, time draws closer to an end this afternoon. It will be difficult for my cat to understand why I'm not back at home six a' clock as usual. In my life, the little things do matter, because they make my life. My philosophy is not to have too much of anything and stay on good terms with time. We should remember stop in time when something is at it's best. I still join you for a cup of tea, but then it's high time to leave and return home. You are really spoiling me taking such a good care of me. Stepping out of a daily routine, might be useful for somebody else. This is not so much the case with a beggar. Once I became used to a beggar's comedian-role, I cannot wind back my life so easily any more.

Why strive for the stars, when luck is so much closer to us. This time I struck lucky with both of you. You are good people who care about others. Don't lose this virtue and you will meet more people who appreciate your company."

"Before we drop you back into town, may I add quickly another discussion point about books, this time? Are you a reader? Judging by your knowledge, you are one, am I right?"

"Books have become my most reliable companions. They keep a useful distance to everything and do no harm. I own only a few books which are essential for me. Most books I can get from the local library. It's good and affordable even for a beggar, that's what libraries are for.

Let me have a look on your book collection. You must love your books, the way you keep them luxuriously stored in book cupboards closed with glass doors. I can see author names I'm very familiar with: Alfred Tennyson - Locksley Hall, Ernest Hemingway / Men Without Women, John Steinbeck / Grapes Of Wrath, Pearl Buck / The Good Earth, Colleen MacCullock / The Thorn Birds, Margaret Mitchell / Gone With The Wind, Patrick White / The Tree Of Man, Bryce Courtenay / Power Of One, Leo Tolstoy / War And Peace, Albert Camus / The Plague, Paul Sartre / Roads To Freedom, Paulo Coelho / The Top Is Lonely, Arundhati Roy / The God Of Small Things, Mika Waltari / Sinuhe The Egyptian, F.E. Sillanpaa, Silja The Maid / Gunter Grass, The Tin Drum / Thomas Mann, Death In Venice/ Johann Wolfgang Goethe, Faust / William Shakespeare, All Is Well That's Ends

Well - nothing could be said better for your invitation than this great testimony of Shakespeare."

"Please take a book for you to read until our next meeting. Which one would you like?" – "I haven't heard yet much about F.E. Sillanpää. To my knowledge, he is a Finnish author. Can I have his book, Silja The Maid? I promise to keep it immaculate. Only looking at a few books, you have indeed a very diverse library. – We better stop now, otherwise I can't make it home in time. I won't remember when I last spoke so much and ate so well. Thank you so much for looking after me, I will always remember you both. The memories of today will help bring more sunshine into my simple beggar-life."

"When you have finished your cup of tea, let's hop into the car and go back to town. If you don't mind, I might as well drop you at your home. This time, Ann has not to come with us. She is meanwhile taking care of the kitchen."

"I hope not to disappoint you when you stop at my modest place."

"Not at all, because you've shown that behind everything is always more than we can see. Don't you worry, rather make sure that we keep in touch and build on our special friendship. Here is also my address and telephone number. – Ann we are leaving now, give Jim a hearty farewell, too. I'll be back shortly."

"You are so good and so nice, God bless you both, even when I'm not too good in religious matters. When you really like me, there shouldn't stand much in your way to see also me and my cat in my home."

"Next time, it will be our turn to come and see you. Don't worry then about cooking. We'll put something together and bring it along with us."

"Now you can sit with me in the front of the car and we can easily talk a bit more to each other. If it's not peak-traffic-hour, by car it is much quicker and more convenient than with the bus. When we do our special shopping in town, once a week, we prefer to take the bus because of all the hustle and bustle to find a parking spot. When we come into the town, please indicate to me how to get to your address."

"Going home, always is quicker. The next corner to the right and we are already at mine and my cat's home."

"Can I come inside with you for just a moment, so that your cat also gets to know me? I wonder what welcome he has for me."

"I've not much to show you. If you are game enough, please follow me."

The door to Jim's only room wasn't fully opened yet and the cat is already at the door, purring happily while rubbing along Jim's legs. He doesn't even stop in front of John, but continues with the cat-welcome.

"You can see, my cat too has accepted you. It is here, where my life after the street continues. It's not a dream-home like yours, but I still like it, because a home is everybody's castle. You are welcome to sit down on my only chair and have a little rest before heading back home. All I can offer you in a hurry, would be a cup of tea."

"Thank you for your kind offer. Another time I'll love to accept also with Ann a cup of tea. Today it's rather late and I better head home in time before late weekend-traffic. You've made up your room quite nice. Size doesn't matter much, if it's homey. I'm off, we keep in touch and please do the same."

"Please tell your wife Ann how much I enjoyed your company, your lovely home and specially her cooking. Drive safely and if it were our destiny, we shall meet happily again. I come out with you and bid you my farewell."

Back in Jim's 'little castle', he finds of a sudden himself rather alone, surrounded by unfamiliar silence. The cat is reminding Jim of his beggar existence. The last daylight is blocked out by the window-curtains, which separate the street-world from Jim's refuge. Another day also for Jim, not another dollar, but more than what money can give.

BEGGAR-CONCLUSION

A 'beggar' too can make an impression. Not all beggars are the same as all the teachers, doctors, plumbers, you name it, aren't the same. When it comes to the little things in life, this is rather the domain of the 'little people'. Let's not forget that only from little things big things can grow.

Who can relate to the majority of little things in a life, finds contentment and happiness easier than on the highway of the big things. A rush is part of big things. To get there, means also, to be more on a collision course with others. A beggar's life is to stay rather away from so said 'collisions'. Why also the 'beggar' belongs to an 'comedian-family', is not difficult to answer: An existence which doesn't ask for great demands, is already the closest one to an 'comedian-role. How the 'comedian-beggar' can still maintain life-quality, is also a matter of balancing bad with good. Here, too, has never anything been only bad or good.

Fewer expectations are the result of a personal insight, which is the key to keep 'bad' versus 'good' in check. A beggar holds this 'key' simply in a simple understanding relative to him, in this story, Jim, because we all act as we understand.

CHAPTER III

TOOLMAKER

I bet, many people would ask themselves: 'the comedian-debate' is shaping slowly but surely up; 'toolmaker' is however something I can't remember having come across yet.

Let's climb our 'notorious social ladder' and find out, where a 'toolmaker' can find his/her place. It won't be at the bottom nor on the top. Not at the bottom, because too much goes into 'toolmaking' to push it down that far. Neither on the top, as this position is well guarded by 'traditional owners'. Who are those owners? They are still today: solicitors, doctors, teachers, politicians and many more, we all know them. The principle of "old habits die hard" serves them still well.

Technology has meanwhile diversified much of the way people are working to such a degree that the 'old habits' lose in a modern society the exclusive justification. Many professions have emerged with technological progress and new knowledge of which 'toolmaking' is only one.

Why is the author selecting here this highly specialised profession of a 'toolmaker'? It has been a starting point in the author's life already more than sixty years ago. Yes, dear reader, you are reading correctly, a toolmaker has the courage to also bring on paper, which doesn't fall short of an ordinary citizen's daily life. Aren't we all ordinary citizens at its best? Isn't the 'holy cow' of education doing also its part, dividing societies? I'm not answering this question here, but rather referring to the 'comedians' whom we cannot escape regardless of our societal stand.

By saying that 'toolmaking' has also been a starting point in the author's life, doesn't mean, this has been the end of the author's road. The author acknowledges that anything done right, perfection not excluded, will lead to the bigger 'picture' in a life. The emphasis is on doing something right, which then should make every person, every work equally important in reality. If we were true to ourselves, we could acknowledge for instance that simply a cleaning work is never one and the same, depending on a personal degree of applied discipline. Here is the key for everything we do: not what we do, but how we do something.

Let me finally get started with the usual day, a toolmaker faces in 'his comedian-role': Five thirty in the morning, the alarm clock goes off as usual during working days. For Michael this includes almost every Saturday. Early in the morning at quarter past six, it is time for him to leave home in order to be at work before seven o'clock.

Why before? Also Michael is expected to start work like everybody else at seven o'clock sharp. It's already here where professional demands start.

But before this part of Michael's life will begin in earnest, the first steps of daily life still take place at home. His wife Sara, twenty eight, gets also so early out of bed. They have been married for a few years and have two little children. A girl, Ann, four years old and the boy, Adam, two years.

Sara works only part-time as a kindergarten teacher, so that she has time enough for her children at home. The children don't see dad in the morning. Long before they wake up in their own bedroom, daily life is already in full swing at home. The bathroom had its 'visitors', however not before both parents engage in a regular, daily light gymnastics on the balcony of their ground floor apartment. They have to be cautious not to disturb their neighbours on the side and above. Breakfast that follows, too is selected to a healthy standard, which consists of wheat-biscuits and milk, a variety of mixed nuts with added currants, one apple, sometimes an orange or banana, a cup of rosehip-tea and the breakfast is complete. While at the table in the dining-corner adjacent to the kitchen, Michael and Sara watch the morning news on TV. They have to turn TV's volume down, not to wake up their children too early. Once in the kitchen the thermos-flask is filled with more tea, two sandwiches ready in a suitable lunch-box, the wall-clock tells Michael that he is on track to leave for work. A hearty farewell to Sara sends Michael on his daily mission to perform as a toolmaker. Not far from the flat, he catches the bus. In case, the bus is running late, the car is then waiting in the garage at home making sure that Michael doesn't arrive late at work.

Organisation to the detail is also the key for toolmaking. It starts already in private life, because no toolmaker can perform with a private life upside down long-term well. To be honest, what every work that performs is asking for, I call a 'back-up' in private life. Excessive drinking, late nights, unhealthy eating habits, stress as a result of not balancing work with individually suitable activities like hiking, swimming, reading and much more, without forgetting family and friends. From a good family back-ground, Michael has learnt enough to continue building positively on his own life.

On the bus, Michael catches up with another work-mate: "Are you ready for another day's battle?" – "Not really, but what other choice have we got as 'comedians'? You know this game of one side taking the responsibility and the other side doing the work." – "It's always the same, nothing new. Neither you nor I are bad off, there are many others who have got more to complain. The end of the day will tell us, how our day was at work." – While talking, the time on the bus passes quickly. The weather plays today its part for a change, so that no umbrella is needed for the short walk from the bus-stop to the tool-company. A well fenced area keeps the operational buildings away from the public.

The gate stops vehicles at the entrance, leaving only passage open for pedestrians. On the way to the change-room, flower-beds in full bloom border the inner court-yard amidst fresh, short kept green grass patches. Residential buildings in the surrounding area do not differ much from the company's buildings. They are all white and clean, have a reddish tiled roof. The company's windows however have the shutters missing. These windows face away from the main road and are bigger than their residential counterparts. Inside, not much light is switched yet on, as the clock still shows ten minutes to go before operations begin in the tool-company, at seven o'clock sharp. Until then, Michael too picks his blue dust-coat in the change room uniformly worn across the whole company. Company rules are here to better streamline work-efficiency. One of them is that every Monday a clean, ironed dust-coat is brought from home to start the week visibly new. Failure to do so, the company reserves the right to send an employee home and return with a proper dust-coat. Michael didn't have any second thoughts on the matter, because also he can see past this rule and experience its benefits.

The basic company building-layout is on three levels. In the basement are located the warehouse and preparation-operations. The first floor holds the reception, one office room only, the by far biggest area is dedicated to the 'toolroom'. Above, on the second floor, is a large recreation area besides the design department. All building floors present a homey atmosphere, not much different from one another. To enter the toolroom however, access is only allowed to persons who know the pin-number of a device on the side of the entrance door The same applies for the design department. Reason for this security measure is that company efforts remain in house and not traded outside.

Already in the reception area, indoor plants welcome everybody. And it doesn't stop there, even between machines, work benches are boxes arranged with magnificent indoor plants not to interfere with toolroom - operations, but embellish also working conditions naturally. The owner's opinion is that nature should not be denied its place with the high-tech business activities. Nature can support us only, if at least reinstated where it has been displaced.

The door to the toolroom introduces everybody into a largely unknown work environment. Despite ten minutes still to go before a general start of a new working day, buzzing noise already fills some areas, where bright ceiling light illuminates green machine-blocks. They vary in sizes along marked pathways. One is a machining-centre, while the other is a latest 'high-speed-machining–centre'. Additionally to the noise from these operations, a typical toolroom-smell is in the air, which originates mainly from coolant-fluids and lubricants from machines. The temperature in the room is controlled by air-conditioning in order to protect the computer systems driving the machines. The machines are linked to other computers in a more sound-proof section right in the toolroom-centre. Glass walls keep this 'brain-centre' closed but not separate and is within everybody's reach.

Computers here are operated by toolmakers to create complex three-dimensional technical models, through 'Solid Works' and then are given tooling paths with tooling-data by another computer system, called, 'Master-Cam'.

Michael has a high-speed machining-centre running over night. He is pleased to see it still running, which means, while he went home, the machine continued working. Time in today's world is declared an important, if not the most important part of modern work operations.

"Who is here now the 'comedian'?" asks Michael him-self from time to time. "The machine or I"? The answer probably is: As long as the cooperation between man and machine works to satisfaction on both sides, neither one of them is the 'comedian, easier said than done, proves the daily reality.

Michael too rotates with the toolroom tasks according to his ability to learn. In times of a shortage of real skilled people, the company has successfully implemented continuous in-house training. Every employee is given the chance to further his/her career within the company. Such a tailored individual learning process keeps the company with the constant demands of changes and progress better on track.

Michael did after his 'Abitur' (matriculation) a full apprenticeship in toolmaking. Since then, instead of going back to a formal further education, which is outside a continued professional career, the company assists also him with in-house and outside training. The benefits are mutual, the company has an answer to an expert shortage, is flexible to changes and last but not least also money remunerates the better efforts of its employees.

All the ceiling lights have turned on at seven o'clock, distributing good visibility into all areas of the toolroom. More machines have started operations. On workbenches toolmakers do the fine-fitting assembly-work on tooling ranging from handy hundreds of kilograms up to ten tonnes. Tools are here not hammer, screw driver, chisel, but sophisticated, complex manufacturing elements, which produce mostly consumer products in a modern industry to a high efficiency and repeatability. Many components out of different tooling make for instance: watches, cameras, videos, TVs, shoes, cars, motorcycles bicycles, ball pens, hair combs, tooth brushes, toys, also automation on production lines go hand in hand with tooling. In other words, one will hardly be able to name something today that isn't made by tooling.

As tooling is so complex, its costs are generally speaking rather on a high side. To make for instance a camera, millions of dollars are going first in tooling, before a finished product will enter the market.

Michael has on 'his machine' a hardened form-part for a fan-blade which will go into a new passenger car, behind a radiator. The machine spins with its high speed an extremely hard tool-bit. It enables to take a minute amount of steel continuously off by following program-med contours. A correct result is after many machining-hours a shiny finish especially in the product area. Much preparation goes in machining ahead and it doesn't stop there. Toolmakers prepare also the different kind of finishes making a product to look nice.

Michael has been with the company over ten years. Not everybody in the company takes part in further training programs, but he does. Only proven practical records become incentives to earn more money. Michael is a quick learner. 'Wonders' can be achieved with the in-house, outside-support and own studies, when the right discipline keeps all parties at one table. The company has a program for this further training.

Not only the owner, but also the technical manager have worked their way up in all different 'comedian-positions'.

The company differs from many others in the area and further around. Its success story is that every employee is equally treated. Team-leaders are nominated to lead in projects an open input from all workmates. 'Murphy's law' and hidden agendas are then less likely to gain the upper hand. Instead of a 'pyramid'-employee-structure, where directions go from the top, everybody here can ask openly for help and consequently learn from each other. Only with a majority-consent a leader is emerging. This is also a constant 'touchstone' to avoid unnecessary mistakes, which can cost a company untold amounts of money.

How is this system accepted by the employees and is it working?

Michael has this to say in a shared discussion with the author: "As we all know, nothing is perfect, especially in a working-world. And if I compare other places with this one, no doubt, where is a will, there is also a way. Who wants, can find a niche in our toolroom, according to his/her abilities. Some are happy to stay with a limited operation which they can perform to perfection easier than moving further up the skill- and knowledge ladder. In the 'Master Cam' and 'Cad-Cam' section work also female employees. They too have done their time in the toolroom before moving on to something where they have been found specially talented. I'm happy with the company. If somebody has a complaint, the 'black-box' near the toolroom entrance is there for written complaints from employees who want to remain anonymous.

Friday, every fortnight, after work, a meeting takes place above the toolroom in the recreation area. A limited amount of beer is free for everybody and any discussion is encouraged, including complaints. Pro and cons are heard in a proper fashion. Decisions are made on a majority consent as long as it does not interfere with the company's 'lifeline'. In a sense, it cannot be denied that in the company we are all somehow 'comedians' of the business. We are given some free play within the company to responsibly contribute to an all over success.

And as nothing is free in this world, everything has its price, too. Generally speaking, so far common sense has prevailed, so that no unreasonable ideas or demands have come forward. I believe, a good leadership has also good arguments ready to be discussed. A few years ago we had a recession which didn't go past our toolroom business, too. Unanimously was then decided that we voluntarily restrict our normal working conditions until business is again out of the 'bottle-neck': no holidays, overtime without pay for the time being, sick-pay referred to company-doctor's appraisal, working hours split between toolroom sections and some more temporary measurements.

When six months later, business turned around again, not only everything was back to normal but losses were also remunerated for the following 6 months stepwise. – I mention this, because it shows the commitment of every employee towards this company. Work and income depend largely on the company's wellbeing. When needed, a helping hand does no harm. Walking away from problems is neither intelligent nor a toolmaker's attitude. Toolmaking itself means attention to details. The details cannot be discussed here, because they are limitless. I can only remember during my apprenticeship our master telling us: if you want to become a good toolmaker, every day should start with the intention to do a better job. Whether we like it or not, work-life has become a 'race' for superiority. The choice is your's, you are in or out. To be in, is better, because the intelligent person can see the dependence of work- and private-life.

Times have changed, no more the 'clever ones' are on one side and the other side is crowded with 'stupidity'. Technological, scientific progress have changed the landscape of intellect-recognition. Many new professions have emerged, demanding complex intellect, of which a broad public only knows little or nothing. I'm suggesting that toolmaking is still one of the many overlooked 'comedian-existences', to put it bluntly, because of widespread ignorance. The traditional scale of doctors, lawyers, teachers, engineers and closer to the 'bottom' 'workers', is not a fair assessment of today's society any more. In a world in which distance is shrinking through technology, all our fates are linked more than ever before. Not integrating but separating views will only continue to foster divisions. 'Silent achievers' can call home at any level of societies' notorious evaluation-scale.

Why I, the author discuss here toolmaking-matters, which could also be related to other qualified professions? It is simply to open the minds of more people, who are eventually comfortably sitting back in ignorance towards a fairer assessment. New ways of reality based thinking are long overdue. I've given Michael here the role to speak out issues, which I, the author, have so far experienced taking place or becoming evident during my seventy seven years. Let me spin the 'wheel' of events a bit further:

A doctor and a toolmaker do not only cover different professional fields, but are considered to be 'worlds' apart. Let's put to the test an intelligent doctor and an intelligent toolmaker to see how far they are really apart.

In most cases, both would have very little understanding of each other's professional field. This does not however mean that their stand in society should continue to differ still in the twenty first century. A surgeon is one of the few in the medical profession who needs to incorporate in his/her professional performance both, as well practical skills as a theoretical knowledge. A toolmaker's theoretical knowledge is on the other hand easily overlooked while focussing mainly on practical skills, which can easier be seen. Isn't always more behind something, what the eye can see?

If somebody disagrees here, he/she does not understand much. No matter what a professional stand, each professsion well done, deserves one and the same respect! The world cannot be any more separated, so that the clever-ones are on one and 'idiots' on the other side. How much is education responsible for this division? Where is a justification of education like it is still practiced today, one leg is hanging on to tradition, while the other one tries to move forward with time? One result of it is also the 'haves' and "have-nots" which is definitely not a measurement of intelligence. More professions today are based on a foundation of the 'little building blocks' with their skills and knowledge. Both skills and knowledge should make them equal partners and not divide them with a top and bottom of a scale.

Let's go back to our test, the intelligent doctor versus the intelligent toolmaker. If both were to start the profession of the other, who would reach first the set goal? It's probably not so much the question of reaching first the goal of the other but rather to give equal opportunities.

Under these conditions it will become evident that most likely both will reach their goal. Then it is again a proof that under equal opportunities equal results can be achieved. During my life I've also heard that candidates for a pilot training are selected with a preference from a toolmaking background. Doesn't this already tell something?

Enough of thoughts! The idea has been, not to lead an isolated discussion here, but to look at toolmaking and compare it with other professions. Much of this discussion leaves something to think about. The author's personal experiences in management positions have on the subject here a foremost bearing.

Many statements are part of a personal success story. Those statements put to the test in the real world have proven not to be simply fantasies but carefully advanced work-improvements.

Decisions were always made with a majority consent of all employees. Don't get me wrong, this is not an 'outcry' of a failed 'comedian-role'. It's rather the opposite, namely how to get out of an uneasy 'comedian-role' as Michael and the author partly have done.

To go deeper into this kind of experiences, cannot be the purpose of the 'comedians'. It is rather suggested to keep one's mind open in an appraisal of other professions. As I've already said: there is always more behind what the eye can see."

Let's go back to Michael's arrival at work and how he starts his new day in the tooling company. Production time is documented on a central key-board of a computer with starting- and finish-time of a job number. Attention is also here requested, because the pay of each employee is automatically calculated and on pay-day transferred into an employee's bank-account.

Besides this organisation, every employee keeps his/her own record book of which the copy goes daily into a central tray, controlled, signed and filed away in case of computer hick-ups.

Michael realizes: "My machine has been good, it worked through all the night." - The result is shaping up. The cutting tool went to the check-post for wear-control three times. The automatic tool-changer supplied a new cutting tool in between, so that the finish-cutting of the fan blade form-segments continued undisrupted.

The surface finish is excellent, not far off from a mirror-finish. The special cutting tool which the machine is spinning at one hundred fifty revolutions per second, is diamond-coated. A light 'stone-finish' needs only to go in front of the diamond finish, supplying then a surface in which you can see your face like in a mirror. Power failure didn't occur either, that's why no production time was lost.

While the machine continues the 'tool paths' Michael had programmed in cooperation with other toolmakers, another task is waiting for him: as he is an appointed team-leader of this tooling project, he assists other colleagues in the preparation of all the other components, which in the end make this tool an injection mould. Time is very important here.

There is no room for mistakes. Everybody has to deliver his/her best, day in day out. Totally open communications between employees is paramount. And yet, in a toolroom it is usually very little spoken. Why this is so, because the drawings are the 'language'. Good preparation deter-mines how the rest is going.

Michael pays the polishing department a visit, informing them ahead of the job coming from 'his machine': "Tomorrow afternoon the first parts will come to your section; all up, you have one week to do your polishing. I'll keep you informed on my progress. The project is an export order to Japan. A cargo-shipment is scheduled for the end of the month, which gives us less than three weeks to finish the job. From next week, we might have to consider extra man-power and extra hours on the weekend to secure this delivery date."

Morning tea-time arrives also today in no time. Not everybody is heading for the recreation room, which depends on the job somebody is on. The 'comedian' is here again the toolmaker. Computers and machines have 'the right of way'. Not everything is however bad about this; to give a helping hand when it is most needed and then again allow toolmakers to 'recharge the battery' are important leadership credentials. When work for instance on the weekend is required, employees who have helped to keep a promised delivery date, have one paid day-off extra the following week. Incentives are the 'carrot' also in work-related issues.

Before Michael takes on another job, 'his machine' continues 'doing the right thing'. He also checks the progress of the other project-components in a close consultation with his team of toolmakers.

Everybody knows that Michael doesn't mind to give a helping hand. 'Bossing-around' is out in the company. Every employee has not only a voice but is asked to contribute with qualified action to an overall better efficiency. Machining, fitting to tolerances of one thousandth of a millimetre and producing a whole range of surface finishes in areas, where it is required; like an already mentioned 'mirror-finish', or 'leather-surface-look' and much more. All this requires a strong mind and physics to learn in a constantly changing high-tech-environment, patience and again patience, what I call a toolmaker-character. Here a stable private life feeds positively on a long-term performance, which shows also in a remuneration. Again an insatiable desire for managing details is characteristic for all qualified work-performance. Nobody should be regarded here the 'comedian' which is however still widely imbedded. The increase in a shortage of long-term experienced toolmakers is a growing problem, like in any other qualified profession. Team work at one and the same 'eye-level' has become the answer and not unjustified employment levels of the 'comedians'. Michael is proud to work for a progressive company. He is highly respected, because the respect between colleagues is mutual. Problems are here to be solved, to keep a cool head, stay patient, so that more than one person can look at possible problems from a distance. We all know that sleeping over a problem can make a difference already next day.

Not all toolroom-businesses are of course progressive. There are also so called 'sweatshops' where a company operates with minimum investment, especially in its people in order to maximize profit. This is the wrong way round to deal with competitiveness or economical pressure.

Shortcuts are not long term sustainable. In some places, toolmakers have to be 'Jack of all trades', which means: bring your own tools, a job is entirely the responsibility of one man. Only in the end the outcome: good, less good or bad becomes often evident. When 'no good' the 'poor bugger' can pack up and try somewhere else his toolmaker-luck. This has then turned into a real 'comedian'- existence.

In reality, not the toolmaker has only become the 'comedian', much the same could be the employer called. Uncertainty in customer satisfaction is a too high price to pay. A long haul with organised quality outcome will convince with time even the best 'cutting-edge-customer'.

In the 'toolmaking-game' it is a known fact that toolmakers with huge toolboxes are often the ones who've worked in 'sweatshops.

Toolboxes usually grow bigger in those places and not smaller. Lack of organisation is to blame for this situation, in which a company not supplying working tools mistrusts its employees in reality.

In 'sweatshops' usually one incentive is offered, namely slightly a better pay. It is supposed to compensate for a lack of organisation an employer as well as employees.

Less perfect tooling keeps also coming back more often for repairs and servicing. It can keep a 'business wheel' spinning. Good toolmaking is doing everything right and have rarely returns. Why this is so, is very simple: efforts and money spent beforehand can secure a better outcome than have to re-invent the 'wheel' afterwards.

Small businesses, like most toolrooms, are the 'comedians' of big businesses. The small ones deliver efficient and competitive work, which the 'big' usually buy in. The 'big' battle politics instead. Watch out 'politics' and do not get caught in interest games. Toolmaking is a different world all together. A straight forward thinking can only deliver in toolmaking. Michael is happy to be on a side of an equation where he can understand his work-life. The known 'comedian' is better than the unknown.

Although toolmaking is the 'comedian' of bigger businesses, 'small' and 'big' still needs each other. The legendary 'small building blocks' created also in toolrooms help make or break a big business.

Especially recently "big" ought to earn its justification only, when employing also 'big'. Different to a smaller business, 'bigger business' seems to swing easier the axe on employees instead of turning the screws on the real causes. Good employees are the life-line of smaller businesses and therefore a matter of greatest importance for a toolroom to stay in business with the 'big' ones.

This excursion into the pro and cons of toolmaking is only a small window of the author's lifetime experience. Much is said, but more is still to be said in the course of a general understanding and not a specialised one. Let's see how this particular day continues for Michael:

In the past years, also Michael has advanced himself with in-house-training, own studies and assistance of the industry-academy in Computer Aided Drawings (CAD) and Computer Aided Machining (CAM). The company supports an initiative of the industry educating the staff in their own academy-set-up in accordance with the fast changing technology. Employees who attend this institution stay employed with a normal pay, but on condition to perform with proven records, which should be regarded fair enough.

One Master-Cam computer terminal is waiting with another project to get started by Michael while his high-speed machining-centre is still running. This is only possible because of his good knowledge and experience 'down to the wire', not to forget a good dose of an ability to concentrate.

The next job is a progression fine-blanking tool. Something which produces fast and economically precision metal components for a video camera.

Michael starts with an operation plan on paper which will be discussed with other colleagues before a go-ahead with the computer design.

Preparation here can be already half the work. On the other hand, it is a waste of time when not enough attention to details is given.

Before Michael can enter deeper into his new task, the lunchtime-bell surprises also him. With all respect, this work is not a bricklayer's job, where a trowel can just be put aside. Michael continues today and has his lunch-break later. He would lose just too much, if he walked away.

The toolroom is maintaining an image not all specialised places are keen to follow. A business will show shortfalls only with time, for whatever reason it cuts short on image-efforts. The toolroom Michael is employed has developed its own philosophy in relation to its employees like its customers: why should our work environment be different from our home, where people like to be? When properly maintained, it doesn't come to a mess and disorder in the first place.

Michael remembers his apprentice master telling: if you want your vernier and you know where it is, you'll have it in a matter of seconds; if the vernier is however not in the place, you start looking for it, and this is a waste of time! The so called 'building blocks' of an efficient work start here, no matter on what level this might be.

Everything that is done right and efficient are the challenges also in toolmaking. The toolmaker looking for the vernier is likely to be the one, who works up a sweat during the day. His performance eventually falls behind the better organised toolmaker, who is the typical slow operating expert, slowly but surely reaching a goal by avoiding rush-mistakes and staying calm without breaking out in sweat.

Another suggestion by the owner: if we can't show our friends or families, I'm not talking here about the company's customers, our work place with pride, then there is something wrong with us! We spend one third of our life in a work place. If the work place is simply nice and orderly, employees, customers, visitors have more confidence in what we do; something good is more likely to feed back goodies.

Michael adds to the philosophy of this company: it can be done, without much effort, when everybody understands all this, playing his role for the benefit of all. Our toolroom is never dirty, dusty or has got any kind of mess. Everything is so well set up and maintained that anything different from it, is crying foul. The floor in the whole building is for instance polished blue epoxy; all free areas and passages are marked with clean, white lines; all equipment is placed on coated metal trays recessed into the floor, so that any liquid spill or metal stays in that area and is not carried around with shoes. Surrounding each equipment are perforated special foot-mats level with the rest of the floor. The foot-mats are designed to prevent foot-tiredness of employees, who stand all day.

To think about positive measures beforehand can help a working process, what has always been better and cheaper than fixing something running out of control.

However, a set-up like this toolroom didn't take place over night. From the early days, now more than twenty-five years ago, the company policy and consequent philosophy was: every day, we do our best in order to improve working conditions, which leads to a better efficiency and product-quality. All this depends also on which market a company plans to serve in the future. To make watches has undoubtedly different requirements from making shoes in a factory. As competition becomes today tighter and tighter, 'high-tech' captures more and more manufacturing, especially when high production-output-numbers are in demand. Here is the best messenger a convincing set-up. Therefore, different markets mean different quality-tooling-requirements. For no other reason, "sweat-shops", high-tech- and many between-toolrooms do exist. And it is good, because toolmakers have then a choice where to join a skilled work-force.

Let's continue with the visit of the toolroom, where also Michael works: The large windows are not only kept clean like it is done in a home, but have also special features: from inside one can look out whereas from outside vision is barred; alarmed windows have become in today's world an unfortunate necessity. Light from the windows mixed with ceiling lights and work-lights near a job, allow a good vision with almost no existing shade.

Plant arrangements in boxes along the toolroom-passages which also lead to the centre, already been mentioned. In the centre is a tooling-office located with numerous tooling cabinets, next to it in a glass-enclosed area are high precision control-instruments, including a computerized measuring-machine as well as a number of optical measuring-microscopes.

All in all, this certainly is a multi-million dollar high-tech toolroom-set-up enabling its employees to operate competitively. For a customer, it is always more convincing what he can see. He is the 'king' and who serves him, has to put up with the 'comedian-role'. This is the all-important rule also for a toolroom. It makes life no doubt easier when one learns to live with those rules.

When busy, time runs always short. And a day in a toolroom is certainly no-different. It's therefore better to like what we do, otherwise we'd waste our and other people's time. It's not good to watch the time as it drags the day along. If we are serious enough, the time during the day should help at work, and not hamper performance. Nothing is worse than an environment of unhappy employees, which can be prevented by a good leadership. Not a 'pyramid' - organisation where a 'lonely top' has the say, but a respectful cooperation in which the rule of thumb doesn't reign, but a readiness to listen to others. Too often, one-sided knowledge leads to mistakes and eventually to conflicts. The traditional hierarchy of a master, manager, boss and so forth has to adapt to team-requirements, where everybody contributes at more or less the same eye-level. A 'leader' is appointed by a majority agreement between the management and employees. Such selection stands as long as a leader satisfies the tasks with appropriate circumspection for requirements of team-members.

Rapid technological progress today and in the future cannot be served any more with its complexity by individuals. Project-knowledge and related risk-factors demand a wider control at every stage of any tooling-process.

Thus the modern demands of a social fairness are not only in a toolroom, but right across all economical activities, including the present sorry-state of financial institutions.

Michael is long enough with the company and has learnt the benefit of openness and not behind closed-door-politics. It doesn't take long to find out whether a new employee fits into the company-team. Openness keeps him/her in the team. On the other hand, inability to listen and cooperate within an existing team will not take long for somebody to give him-herself the marching order.

Although more can be said about aspects of toolmaking. It still comes down for Michael to 'touch ground with his both legs', when he spends his day with toolmaking. The forgoing discussion should be seen as a wider contribution to the 'toolmaking-game'. The author's toolmaking experience of a lifetime can only contribute to the "comedian-toolmaker'. There are certainly people who can connect to what has been said and others, who wonder about it, because we all tend to live in an isolated 'glass-house' and know very little about other professions. The undertaking of this book is about shedding 'light' into some of our professional 'holy-cows'.

How far has Michael's 'ground-touching' in a toolroom brought him forward today? He decided to postpone his lunch-time in order to start with a design-layout for a next project. He wanted to discuss with other colleagues the first basic ideas on paper after their return from the lunch-break. Toolmakers mainly with a proven experience have emerged with time in a qualified discussion within the company.

Three other toolmakers with many years design-experience join Michael in the CAD-section constructively scrutinizing the start of a project.

Michael leaves his sketches with them so that they can enter into a better prepared discussion, while he takes his lunch-break two hours later in the recreation-room. A call home on the mobile only from the recreation-room keeps the family in touch. And both sides know, everything is fine as well at home as at work. The company allows Michael an extra fifteen minutes, because he had his lunch later. The discussion starts straight away, when he returns to the CAD-section.

Other points are also discussed so that the next move on the CAD-terminal can go ahead. Michael has to be very well organised operating the CAD-system and at the same time to keep the high-speed machining centre running, help supervising progress on the preparation-and assembly stages. All this sounds too much for one person. It's not the case, because there are also others ready to assist. Nobody is left on his/

her own. A 'burden' carried responsibly on more than one employee's shoulders, is less than half the trouble. A good leadership is here again the key. In case of arguments, a company-rule is to meet outside the toolroom and if needed, 'knock heads together 'for goodness' sake.

The first hours of the afternoon pass quickly, almost unnoticed, at least for Michael. And he is not alone. The end of a standard eight hour working day is shown on a centralised wall-clock. The job-cards of all employees go into a box at the entrance of the supervising office after receiving the day's final stamp of the time-clock. Here are no loud siren-sounds announcing either a beginning or end of a day. Still before three thirty in the afternoon, the Master-Team-Leader goes around in the toolroom briefly discussing the need of additional time, who should stay back and on which project. There is an unwritten rule that a good toolmaker is expected to work extra time. For that reason, most employees know whether or not their extra time is required. As time in the toolmaking business is most important, also Michael has almost never worked 'bricklayers' hours' where time tells when to put the trowel aside. In a modern toolroom - industry quality and price are covered by know-how and efficiency as a matter of course. The time of a project delivery is however strictly binding, if a business wants to survive. Time is money, particularly in a toolroom. As long as Michael can remember, he has been working on Saturdays, too, with the exemption of one Saturday per month in order to catch up with life outside and family.

Today on a weekday, Michael has been back from two-thirty in the afternoon on the high-speed-machining-centre in order to change a set-up of hardened parts for the fan-blade injection mould. A fourth year apprentice-toolmaker watches Michael first before he receives step by step instructions to help with the set-up. Michael leaves a clear instruction not to start the machine, before he returns from the assembly section. When Michael returns, he tells the apprentice to explain what he has done. Michael then checks himself closely communicating with the apprentice what was done. Everything is then ready to go, the moment of truth comes when the computer starts the machine while the fingers are still on the 'speed-button', only turning it gradually higher. Behind the machine's safety transparent enclosures eyes can watch how the machine starts the new program. The apprentice is praised for his efforts. He is the next generation of toolmakers. The better he is trained, the earlier he can step in and work in a team responsibly. Michael knows too well that leading a team means to share responsibilities and not do everything yourself.

This is only possible in an environment, in which respect and trust are firmly established. An insecure employee will not voluntarily entrust on one hand his knowledge and skills to others, on the other hand, it would be short-sighted to keep everything close to the own chest.

Experience shows that people acting like this, really have most of the time only little to hide. An open-minded team-toolmaker learns in a constant competition, so that he/she has not to worry falling behind strong-emerging employees. This is however a subject to a leadership talent. Because of high discipline and know-how requirements in a toolroom, toolmakers have a special level of sensibilities. Patience is a toolmaker-virtue. The patience can last surprisingly long, but when reaching its limit, it can explode much to anybody's surprise. If this happens, the calm of other team members remains the highest order not to unsettle a colleague even more. Michael recalls such an event occurring only recently: A colleague who had been with the company for forty years, walked off the job all of a sudden, for no apparent reason. All those years, he was regarded "the still water running deep". Something, perhaps in his private life, must have triggered 'this still water' to become a 'torrent'.

Private and work-life cannot be regarded separately. One goes inseparably with the other. Private problems feed negatively also here onto work performance. Though, work cannot be regarded a charity organization. The 'trick' is balancing private- with professional life. What others don't know, they can't help. Therefore a leadership has also a door at work, where concerns other than direct work-related ones can gain a hearing. This is best done not directly at work for practical reasons.

A good night's sleep can attain that little distance, what is a proven measure in any kind of conflict. The effect of such a distance cannot be underestimated: everything looks with hindsight at least like half the trouble. The 'troubled' person regains this way the necessary confidence to go back to work, because no one has lost his/her image in the process.

In a few words: Michael was the closest to this incident and followed the colleague to the toolroom-exit;" it can't be that bad that we can't talk it over. Let's go into the recreation room."

"Mind your own business, leave me alone!" Was the answer, Michael received. – "Well, when you don't want help right now, there will be another, better moment. Take care of yourself."

Michael saw the manager, briefly reported what happened and that was that. The manager's answer was:

"Not much we can do, let's wait and see what the day tomorrow will bring. Do you know our 'mate' well enough to pay him a visit later in the day and have a beer in the pub together? Here I contribute twenty bugs to a worthwhile mission, a beer in the local pub. Your effort should help him to get back, where he is usually comfortable.

You have the time off on another day, which you are going to spend tonight helping to sort out what seems to be a problem for one of our valued colleagues. Thanks Michael, you do the right thing, good luck on our mission! Take my phone and ring your wife, so that she can also agree. I'll leave you with it."

Because Michael has time off on another day, his wife was at ease with the handling of the evening's outing.

Michael did stay back another hour on the CAD system to allow some more time before visiting the colleague's home. Best intentions are never said to work. And so was it also this time. At the colleague's home, the door did not open completely. Only a rebuff came from inside: "There is nothing to talk!" – Michael said also a few words before the door shut again: "I'm not curious, don't get me wrong, I'm here as a friend to offer my help. You've got my telephone number. When you feel better, why don't you give me a call?"

Michael's family is happy to see him earlier at home. The two children receive first Michael's undivided attention: a hug, a few nice words, questions to encourage the children to tell dad how their day was.

First later, Michael has a word with his wife about the colleague.

When the family sits together at the table for dinner and the workday seems to have become a distant memory, the phone rings.

"Is that him?" – Michael thinks for a moment. – "I go into the other room, the children don't need to listen to what is said on the phone this time around. – Yes it's me, Michael, I'm glad you ring. How do you feel now?" – "The reason for my call is that I feel sorry being caught short as you came around my home to see me. I thought again over your words and want to thank you so much for looking past somebody else's problem. I'll promise to be back tomorrow. To barricade at home with a problem won't help anybody. I rather return to my daily routine and not let problems take over my life. It has been long brewing. I took however a wrong turn, of which I became aware the moment you stood in front of my house door. I know now that I have good friends also at work. It should help balancing problems at home. Only when we are in such a situation, we realise the importance of both, private- and work-life to be in harmony with each other. We can't choose our family, but our friends. And specially friends can help with a wake-up call at the right time. We both have better a good night's sleep and don't keep talking. First thing tomorrow morning I'll see the manager and sort out what is needed. With regard to you, I thank you so much for your support. We and our families should have shortly a get together." – "I'm so pleased that everything could turn for you back to normal in such a short time. Be strong and remain our good toolmaker and friend whom we know already for so long. See you tomorrow."

One work-day is almost over also for Michael. The next day will be another one, a new challenge in an underdog-existence. What remains constant, is to battle for a living. The bright spots of life are unfortunately short-living. They are however worth the much longer battle for such rays of hope.

No day is the same, whether at work or not. At work, performance has to be kept up, because a business in the 'real world' can only flourish on a daily basis with constant renewed efforts. This topic has so far allowed a window into daily work-life of the toolmaker Michael.

How does life after work look for Michael? During the week, little time is left for other interests outside work. Private life is however asking for attention, too. The need of work for a living should not make private life another 'comedian'. We all work to live and don't live to work. Everything has to be here in a balance to each other, the work- and private life. This means that too much or too little work on one side will ask for compensation from another side.

Michael follows here the traditional family-way: he is the main bread-winner and his wife looks mainly after their home and children. A burden on parents' shoulders is this way shared. When Michael comes home from work, the family can spend so more time together.

Work-life doesn't stop at home, even if it is different from that outside. Skills can beneficially cover both sides of life, work and private. It saves time and money while doing everything yourself.

As Michael is also a practical man or better known 'a Jack of all trades', even little time enables him to fix anything in their flat and if needed, on the car, too. The family is already looking forward to building in coming years a house of their own. A lot of good, mutual plan-ning within the family has to precede such a courageous undertaking. They strongly believe that self-help is the best help. To make it happen, one has to be in a good health and strong enough.

Friday is usually the day the whole family pays a visit to the local indoor swimming pool when Michael returns from work. Swimming has become their favourite sport. Most 'worries' from previous days 'swim away' in the heated pool, helping restore mind- and body-energy specially before the weekend. The weekend has arrived and Michael has Saturday off from work, this is then the time also Michael's family can do more what they like. A work-life doesn't leave much time for something else, when considering we work one third of our life, sleep another third and have one third left for something else.

A good organisation which is supported by some degree of fitness is also the answer to best manage a leisure-time. This is of course up to everybody what to do after work or not to do. Michael belongs to that kind of people who use work-discipline also outside work at least partly. It enables him simply to plan in little steps something for his every family-member.

Shopping on a Saturday, has a certain priority. What cannot be bought during the week, is easier selected with a bit more time on the weekend. Michael's wife takes care of the groceries with their daughter, while Michael buys with their son materials needed for the maintenance of their home and the family car. Other acquisitions like clothes, furniture and hobby-gear, if not made by themselves, the family usually purchases together.

A haircut doesn't take weekend-time away, because Michael's wife is doing it at home for the two children and her husband regularly during the week. This helps to save on the weekend time and money. She is the only one who has to see the hairdresser from time to time, which she does during the week. Time for other interests is eventually found after all these necessities have been covered. What kind of interests they might exactly have, mostly depends on the weather. Sunshine is the best time to enjoy outdoor-activities. In summer the children are the ones who want to play in the public pool of the town where they can meet some of their friends out of the neighbourhood. Mum is always with them, whereas Michael uses some of his leisure time to work at home undisturbed instead.

To visit family and friends fills quickly the weekend timetable. All what's left, are a few hours dedicated to a more or less rest, watch a movie later in the day and also give creativity a chance. The children are encouraged to complete a colouring book, make their first steps to learn numbers and letters and together with mum practice a recorder.

What else can fit into a weekend? To visit a church has become also for Michael's family a distant memory. They will eventually find out later in their lives that religion too is an essential part of a cultural tradition.

To abandon tradition equals losing a past. On the other hand, attending occasionally a soccer-game goes easier at a present and Michael is no exemption here. Michael's wife however stays with the children away from these mass-gatherings. She believes that also her two children will find out soon enough whether they want to follow more in the footsteps of their father, mother or both.

Time has always been regarded precious and will remain so. The choice what to do and not, is ours', especially with our leisure-time. Only so much can be squeezed into any time that it won't set us back with stress, personal- and material-losses. To manage little things well has always been better than taking on too much and have to learn to accept the inevitable set-backs.

The exemption of a pub-visit with his mates every now and then, keeps the door open to all others. The main thing for Michael remains his family. His wife leads wisely the family with 'let it be' keeping at the same time her eyes on everything. This doesn't bother Michael, because they trust each other and therefore he loves his family. Whether a friendship or family, the ups and downs in life are best overcome with listening to each other and not to take a single stand.

When the children from next-door come around Michael's place, the toy-box is pulled out from under the bed and specially the Lego-blocks draw the children's attention. Houses, fantastic creations on wheels, animal-reconstructions, monster-figures and all else what children can think of is built jointly or in a competition. Mum has always to keep an eye that the children won't start a fight. Learning such lessons cannot start early enough.

A busy day never fails to make also Michael's family tired and seek bed-time early enough. Here is all well too, that ends well. Not however before the house is put back into a reasonable order, so that another day can start again well for Michael's family. The children need usually a helping hand from their mother to get their room back into a running-order. And when all this is over, mum joins the children in their room with a book. While she alternately sits on a bedside, not much reading-time is needed until both children fall asleep. The light switched off ends the day for the children. Not much later it's bed-time also for Michael and his wife.

'Only the early bird will catch the worm' on another comedian-day.

TOOLMAKER-CONCLUSION

How could the outcome of a troublesome day be better than this?

Toolmaking is by its nature 'problem-solving'. It takes many years to become a 'master' of solving toolmaking-problems. No wonder that toolmakers with long standing experience are becoming a rare 'commodity'. In a progressing world, everybody seems to grab the easier, 'better' professional avenues. Therefore it comes at no surprise that also toolmakers go down that avenue. Technical progress has not yet made toolmakers obsolete. Their numbers have if anything dwindled, increasing the demand for real good toolmakers with broader skills and knowledge. No matter how well and far computers might develop further, the crucial initial as well as final decisions to make a manufacturing process work, will remain with the toolmaker. The more technology tries to take a dependence on skills away, the more expensive becomes the remaining toolmaking. In one sense, this helps lift the 'toolmaker-comedian-situation'. The one who is flexible enough, can learn a lot and earn good money today and in the future-toolmaking.

It is already happening that a toolmaker-reputation is rising from an widely unknown past 'battle-ground'.

Toolmaking and the people behind is a window into a progressing real world. And yet it is surprisingly little known about the profession itself.

Through our education most of us tend to live isolated from other professions. To me, this is a relict of the past. Michael is born into a time of rapid changes. He has mastered it and is moving up into a society's middle class with a necessary new understanding. His toolmaker-comedian-role is lifted on the scale of a social ladder.

Long standing performance will make it through to a recognition in a matter of time anyway.

CHAPTER IV

DOCTOR

Let's climb again our 'social-ladder' higher in the next chapter and see how 'Doctors of Medicine' live in this 'thinner air'. Nothing is really new about a life on the 'top', only that it is 'lonely'.

This doesn't usually happen by accident to arrive on 'top of the social ladder'. It's the people here again, who want to see a doctor higher up than they regard themselves, because of widespread ignorance.

Let's see how a day of a medical doctor compares with other 'comedian-days', and how he/she is coping with such a position.

Has a doctor also to listen to a 'higher authority', which sees him/her in the 'same boat' with the 'comedians'?

Historically, doctors are bound by an oath of Hippocrates to serve one purpose, namely to help preserve life. Doctors have traditionally been in the forefront of all human social ranks, not far from the clergy. The one who can help the suffering of human-body, mind and soul, is in a strong position to exercise power of knowledge over ignorance, too. How could it be otherwise that 'where is bright sunshine, there is inevitably the dark side of shadows. The controversy which is born out of it, is the key to the 'comedian-role' also for doctors. Nobody is spared such oppositions and temptations. During more recent history other fields of human activity claim the title of a 'doctor' for outstanding formal achievements, too.

This chapter is restricted to a 'comedy' of medical doctors.

Not that long ago, verbal or written criticism of the medical establishment entailed prosecution by the authorities or even the death penalty. The French writer and dramatist 'Moliere' escaped diplomatically prosecution in the seventeenth century. He heightened awareness of the medical profession in his comedies, for instance in,

"The doctor in spite of himself" ("Le medecin malgre lui", 1666)

a) Extract one: A medical examination.

   Professor: What do you do with a sick patient?

   Student: Bloodletting.

   Professor: And what are you doing when the patient isn't sick?

   Student: Bloodletting.

   Professor: What is your answer when the patient is rich?

   Student: More bloodletting.

   Professor: What is done when the patient is not getting better?

   Student: If he is poor, don't waste your time; but if he is rich, let repeatedly more blood.

   Professor: You have answered everything correctly, passed the examine and are now a doctor.

b) Extract two:

   "The doctors are only educated enough to give fancy Latin names to the things they do not comprehend. They will kill their patients with the best of intentions, but they will still be dead. All one can do is rest and let nature take its course. All of his previous doctors contradict everyone saying his doctors were idiots, while he blames his one arm for taking up all the nutrients, so he could have it amputated so as to make his other arm stronger".

Today in the new Millennium of 2000, progress in medicine has diversified the task of a doctor beyond the limitations of the past. To cover the many new medical fields, medical doctors had to specialise themselves, too. In the course of this 'comedy' only a few medical professionals are highlighted, so that the humour of a comedy doesn't lose its role in a professional maze.

These are the doctors who have a say about their 'comedian-role' in this 'comedy:

Mr./Mrs. Family-Doctor, 'Pill-Pusher', 'Mouth-Plumber', Witch-Doctor, Surgeon and Flying-Doctor.

Let's pick one at the time and 'roll out the red carpet' for him/her.

It needs also to be said that today's "Pill-Pusher" has been in the past the "Family Doctor". The progress has distanced the two from each other.

First a window into the former

1.) FAMILY-DOCTOR

If no emergency called the doctor during the night, the time to get out of bed is a more convenient day than an early dawn-light affair.

Curtains and window-shutters have only to be opened to let daylight creep into all corners of the doctor-couple's bedroom.

"What day of the week have we got, Anna?"

"Yesterday was a Wednesday, so we must have Thursday today."

"You are a clever woman, no wonder that you are my dear wife! I better see today the bathroom first.

A couple of local home-visits are scheduled for today before my surgery opens at ten am. Not much time is left from now on. My receptionist will be at the surgery in time as usual.

To see patients personally in their accustomed home-environment is a good thing, but what is not so good, is that on those visiting occasions I can't be sure when exactly to return to my surgery. I've to admit that my patients have to learn the waiting-game in the meantime.

Well, actually I shouldn't say that, because we know more than enough about our 'day-in', 'day-out-game'. We doctors can serve only one person at the time. I better stop talking and start my day.

Can we still have breakfast together? It depends on you how quick you are. Can you check the letter-box for today's newspaper? It's good to know what is going on outside our medical-world and why doctors are so busy fixing people's health.

Our younger generation is better to get up, too. School is their current life-lesson, which they shouldn't miss for their own sake. Please keep your eyes on them, before you join me in the surgery. You are our Interior-family-Minister while I'm trying to cover the Exterior-Minister's position. We are more than in one way the "comedians" of what we aim for."

Short after eight a.m., doctor Robert pulls his car out of the garage and joins the early rush-hour-traffic on his way to home-visit number one. Four more visits follow that morning within the town's suburbs.

What all these visits have in common, is that doctor Robert is gaining with each personal visit a broader picture of a patient in his/her familiar environment: "Oh I'm so glad that the doctor has come to see me. It makes me feel so much better. The pain in my chest is however still waiting to be properly examined by you, doctors. I can only hope it's nothing too serious. If I don't make it, who is looking after this place which I call home for over forty years? My neighbour across the road, which I know by the way longer than I can remember, told me that her husband also had this chest-pain and only two days later, he all of a sudden passed away. I don't want that happen to me, please help me in the name of the almighty God".

"Don't you worry, I've looked after you already for many years and it never was so serious that we couldn't get rid of what concerns you. It shouldn't be so easy to pass away."

"You are my saviour, I don't know how to thank you."

Worries and some obvious stress of the patient can indicate to the experienced doctor that eventually a 'bug' has entered the patient's system leaving him/her open to weakening symptoms. Doctor Robert doesn't only describe the appropriate medicine, but also strongly recommends a rest-time in bed and to forget about all the worries. As a family-doctor he has collected not only medical information but also a certain family-history from previous visits to other family- members.

Knowledge out of both fields enables a doctor to better diagnose a patient's condition.

Time is waiting for a doctor neither. Doctor Robert knows by experience already too well that he never makes it back in time to his surgery. More patients in the waiting room are then seeking the doctor's attention. The family-doctor experiences here the moral conflict between 'can and want'. It really doesn't matter if patients more or less sick, they all expect to be regarded as the most important patient of a doctor. They often convince themselves, nobody else suffers like they do. And here the doctor 'finds himself in the midst of a pie' a pie', simply difficult to 'digest'. To do the right thing for everybody, is indeed a task close to impossible even for a doctor.

And how do doctors manage such a challenge? The answer is, "to separate the wheat from the chaff". Also doctor Robert would listen to all what patients have to say but not necessarily seriously. The time in the waiting room for instance sends some patients on a nervous 'down-a-valley-tour'. Doctor Robert knows how to settle patients with his calm and confidence- building. "A broth is never eaten as hot as it is cooked."

From the waiting room a few patient-yarns: Patient 'one' breaks the silence and speaks to his next 'fellow-sufferer' patient 'two': "Today the waiting makes me even sicker. If you knew how bad I feel, I'm not wishing somebody else to experience what I'm going through."

Patient 'two' responds: "It's probably only luck that we don't know everything. I bet you don't want to know what I'm going through."

Patient 'one': "What is it? You make me feel sorry for you."

Patient 'two': "The world is no good any more; no wonder that we all get sick of it. The pain is now in my whole body. I hardly can lift my arms anymore and the walking makes me very quickly tired. I wonder what the doctor has to say and whether or not he can help me."

Patient number 'three' picks up some of this conversation and joins happily in: "You are quite right, I was much better last year and only God knows why I'm again so bad. All this tal-king about the environment doesn't make life any better. I'm sick and tired listening to our politicians how they mislead us. No wonder that we get sick of all this. What do you think?"

Patient 'one' raises his voice, so that the other two can understand him better: "You are not wrong! But what could all this talking be good for, when we cop the suffering anyway? The world will never change; the poor 'buggers' like us get poorer, while the rich get only richer. Where has justice gone these days?"

Patient three spins the yarn further: "Has somebody else heard what is going to happen with the new hospital? It's supposed to be far out in the west. How for God's sake somebody sick like me can get there without a car?"

Patient two enters the discussion: "Haven't you heard about the Ambulance-Service?"

Patient three responds:

"The Ambulance is good and fair, but 'Murphy's law' doesn't stop with them. If you need one, it's usually busy somewhere else. The paramedics also reckon if it's not urgent, you can wait that bit longer. How would they know about the urgency of a call? They tell you, 'the sickest first served'. All you can hope is that you are not sicker than their sickest and for that reason won't make it to the hospital in time." - This yarn keeps spinning in the waiting room. A few more waiting patients join the tittle-tattle, when the doctor's assistant announces: "There will be unfortunately a delay, because the doctor was called to an outside-emergency. We'll however continue to see every-body of you as soon as the doctor is back. I thank you for your understanding and patience." – Time in the waiting room goes more or less unno-ticed while this 'entertainment' goes on. This is one way to make the best out of a 'waiting-game'.

Meanwhile other patients join in the 'waiting –game', mostly the ones who didn't seek refuge in newspapers and magazines of the waiting-room.

Other patients had this to say: "Before the doctor will call a patient again, I think, I have something important to say, too. When I was younger, I can't remember to have seen waiting-rooms of doctors so filled up with sick people like today. It was the doctors who came to see patients at home. Because of that, doctors were called 'family-doctors'. Now, every-thing is different; too many patients and too busy doctors. I wonder, where all this will end up."

"People get sicker and doctors busier. We can all see that. I wonder whether doctors know why it is so."

"In my insignificant opinion, it is all about our way of living. We get what we deserve."

"Excuse me, how dare you say so? Do I for instance deserve to be so miserable because of my poor health?"

"I didn't mean to upset you, but what else could it possibly be that so many of us are here today to see a doctor?"

"I remember my father saying, in the 'old days' we had little and were content. Fewer people were then sick. Nowadays we've much more and can never have enough. Is that why we are sicker?"

"Who knows the right or wrong answer? Our choice is clear, we need to get healthy again with and without doctors."

The moment the doctor calls for the first patient, almost unanimously everybody breathes a sigh of relief.

"It can't take any more too much time for my turn to see the doctor", people in the waiting room eventually think by themselves.

"What can I see?" – Opens the doctor his address. "My dear Paul, you look so much better than on your last visit! You must have done your 'homework' right. Despite the unexpected delay of my emergency-call, you are no doubt coping quite well with the situation. It tells me that we are getting on top of your treatment.- There is enough reason to be positive. How about a joke to cheer us up? A joke makes us forget temporarily the serious sides of life of which we can't do much anyway.

Come what may. Today we can laugh, so let's not miss this opportunity:

'What is the difference between a hill and a pill?- One is hard to get up and the other is hard to get down'. Remember,laughing is always good for our well-being."

The patient hesitantly responds: "I wish you were right, but I still feel down after my accident."

The doctor calmly reassures his patient: "So far your recovery has progressed very well. Don't forget where you were only a month ago. Your help is as important as mine. Let me perform another thorough examination on you and you know then where we stand.

Keep your head up and we are going to win the 'battle'."

Short after midday, Anna, doctor Robert's wife, joins her husband in the surgery. So far, Robert couldn't find a moment to have his cup of morning-tea. Anna is a registered nurse and when their two children are at school, she assists Robert with many medical procedures for a few hours in the afternoon. It is indeed a great help for everybody in the surgery, so that not even Robert cannot forget with a much earned short break to keep his head up during long hours on duty. The time during the day is however flying almost unnoticeably in and outside doctor Robert's surgery. He is often taken in the afternoon by surprise finding that the sun has already shrouded the outside world into twilight while the surgery remains in bright daylight with artificial light. By then his wife Anna has left for their home in order to be with their children when they get back from school.

Doctor Robert picks up the 'Intercom' in order to find out with the receptionist how many patients are still in the waiting room. All he is hoping for, there are not many of them anymore. Even to finish the day early in the surgery, happens rarely before six o'clock pm. Not much time for something else seems to be left then. Doctor Robert, for some reason, finds always time for an urgent after-hour patient-visit. On the way home, he usually likes to do a little shopping on his own. When arriving at home, dinner is mostly waiting already for him.

"Please turn the TV down and tell me how was your school-day. Did the teacher know his lesson? And how about you both? Enjoy school while you can. You will learn early enough that school was the best time in our lives. – Anna, tonight I've got something special organised not only for you but for both of us. Guess what it is?"

"You make me curious, I can't wait, tell me what it is."

"Since 'Mozart' is your favourite composer, 'The Magic Flute' is on stage in our theatre tonight. My receptionist was so kind and organised three tickets for tonight's performance. I knew you have no objections for us three to enjoy together something else but the daily surgery. Get the kids into their beds. They can watch a movie of your choice tonight for a change. What do you think?"

"I always knew, you are not only a good 'family-doctor' but also a good husband, who does not forget his family and the people battling daily with you in the surgery. I'll be ready in half an hour, is that good enough?"

"My Dear, this leaves for us plenty time to attend tonight's event. I also might give my sister a call and ask her, if she can come over to stay with the kids, while we are away. She will be the next in line to receive a ticket to share with us a worthwhile event."

"When somebody is right, it's always you. No wonder why you are such a good doctor and family-father. I really love you from day one."

Occasions like a theatre visit bring the doctor-team also together with other people than the sick one. A doctor-comedian-role receives here a window-view into higher, less burdened fields. As a local doctor, his family is held in high regard by tradition anyway. To keep in touch with a local community requires also from a doctor to be in contact with others. With all due respect, it is an art to step down from a given higher position and not lose ground with other parts of the community.

In the theatre, the doctor-team enjoys seeing familiar and not so familiar faces. This is for them an opportunity to meet people in an more open environment, because daily duties can restrict everybody in their own yard. Refuelling with pleasure, helps tackling another day better. Anna, the doctor's wife cannot anything else but connect to some of the melodies first in her mind. She almost forgets herself and tunes in with her brilliant voice. Robert, her husband holds her hand firm, signalling to her that he likes the performance, too.

The theatre visit has become specially for the doctor-team a late night, because all of them had already a full working day behind.

No wonder that after the theatre performance nothing else was on their minds but to get home for some sleep before the early hours of the new day move in. An event on a weekend leaves however time to extend the evening with a visit to a restaurant.

On the way home, the doctor and his wife drop with their car the receptionist off at her home.

The days of Family-Doctor Robert and his family are no doubt busy. Their after-work-pleasure doesn't however stop with the occasional theatre-visit. There is more on their minds than that namely, their two children ask for undivided attention, also direct and extended family want their share of attention and shopping has to be done to keep the family-home as well as the surgery going. Hobbies like swimming, reading books, hiking, practising music, holidaying, all this wants to be squeezed into doctor Robert's time-table, too. One could almost ask, 'do doctors never fall sick'? Well, besides the fact that they know in most cases how to deal with diseases, doctors are neither safe from catching a cold nor diseases from sick patients. Prevention is here the answer and doctors prove that they are right.

And when a doctor gets sick, a rule covers also him/her: "Birds of a feather flock together" which means, doctors assist each other. In most cases a patient-doctor is receiving medical assistance free of charge.

Not many will argue over that as long as doctors' performances compare with the rest of a society. Also doctors' words cannot 'hold water' unless the words are followed by actions which prove to be in the end right.

The moral obligations attached to a doctor's appointment leading to positive results, is what puts a doctor for more than one good reason into a higher rank of a social ladder in a society. If this is however not given, not even a doctor is any different from other professional fields.

"Bad" doctors wouldn't make much difference to 'bad" plumbers or any other professions. Education can give also 'tools' to a doctor, enabling him/her to start in the 'performance-race'.

Ultimately it's also here not the 'formal-education', making a 'good' doctor but how far he/she can further his/her own education that lead to a sustainable progress.

Doctor Robert's typical day is over. Other days might follow a similar pattern which will only indicate that our habits make us the 'comedians'.

THE FAMILY-DOCTOR-CONCLUSION

A doctor who is reading this 'comedy' should not forget to look at this 'mirror' from not too close. Some doctors might have a smile in their faces, others even might argue the way a 'comedy' opens a broader discussion.

Aren't we living educated in 'glasshouses' of our own, much in an isolation from other 'glasshouses'? Not much is known about the other' glasshouses' and their professsional 'inmates'. Too many of us are still today preoccupied to secure our own 'insecurity' towards the unknown of other 'glasshouses'. Self-esteem, society-ranks, even 'battles' on all imaginable levels have traditionally given a helping hand in order to protect 'glasshouses' with their 'inmates'; don't throw stones against 'glasshouses' and upset its 'inmates', is the 'glasshouse-rule'. 'Inmates' have otherwise to come out of their safe declared territory and eventually learn, what the real world outside their 'glasshouses' looks like.

Some might find this an unreasonable demand. To get accustomed to have a look into one's own 'mirror' has always been a matter of time only. Time has been, still is and will remain man's most valuable asset. Its 'healing forces' should also be taken into consideration by doctors.

Where time has gone missing, whether by doctors or not, human efforts are doomed to fall short. Every shortfall in efforts brings us closer to the 'comedian-doctor', too.

A final admission to this chapter might be that nobody can win every time in a daily life, which is already an abyss for the 'comedian'.

Therefore we all are from time to time more or less 'comedians'.

2.) 'PILL-PUSHER'

How would a day's 'cat walk' of a "Pill-Pusher" look like?

The alarm-clock is set off before it can ring. A new day is beginning for the 'pill-pusher-doctor'. It's early in the morning, the sun hasn't yet cleared the horizon, still shrouded in mist patches.

Toiletry is the first quick action. After that breakfast of one or two muesli-bars follows which are washed down with an instant cup of coffee. Hectic is on. The wife and two kids are still in bed when the house door closes behind doctor Billy. On the streets people are already busy moving up and down on foot and in noisy cars. Billy joins comfortably in his flash Mercedes this general rush-hour. When he arrives in the town's shopping centre, a number of minutes is still left before the opening of the medical centre.

Billy has no parking problems as the medical centre provides him and his other colleagues their own underground parking facility, away from traffic congestion and curious eyes. A stair-way from the under-underground-garage leads through a door directly into Billy's consulting room. Everything is set up jointly with other doctors to save time, so that more patients can be seen. The receptionists and nurses have started half an hour earlier in order to set up medical facilities ready to be used when the daily 'patient-onslaught' begins. Before this is going to happen, Billy uses the time for a friendly opening-chat with his medical staff: "A good morning to all of you, Denise, Kaitlin, Christine, doctor Beatrice and doctor Edward! I'm pleased to see that you all want start another day with me. Yesterday is gone. It's a new day today. Let's make it a good day for all of us. When you are ready, we meet again quickly in our meeting room to discuss today's program. Any question, personal or not, better see me now in my consulting room before the 'sluices' open and the daily 'storm hits' us in our medical centre.

Can we surpass yesterday's patient numbers? Yes we can! Let's get started."

Patients have already arrived in the waiting room. It's now a matter of making the 'conveyor belt' to work: three patients are called at a time. Each one of them is directed into a room of his/her own. A doctor and a nurse briefly welcome a patient, establishing on a laptop necessary data in order to access medical records from the medical centre's data-base.

Questions are asked, pulse and blood pressure are taken, the stethoscope connected to doctor's ears is listening to unfamiliar sounds from chest and back, open your mouth-show your tongue-say 'ah', neck is examined for swellings by finger-touching, walk straight up and down to the door, can you bend down and to the side? Quick eye- and ear-inspection follow, and one final routine test becomes the reflex-test on the knee-front with a little rubber mallet.

One 'picture' of a patient is clear from now on, everything else is also addressed as long as a visiting time allows it. A referral to a specialist, medical prescription shrouded in a 'secret' terminology are still squeezed into a patient-consultation. 'Special' patients can see doctor Billy in his consultation room after the routine-examination.

Confirmation and assurances are for an extra 'special charge' latest here available. At the end of the consultation a patient ought to be contented enough and agree to another appointment with the medical centre. Both, a patient and doctor have an interest to achieve something, even on different terms: the patient is seeking medical help, while doctors with their support basis like to see patients returning for more than one reason. Who would otherwise help a doctor drive his 'Mercedes' and eventually 'bargain' a generous holiday-support from a pharmaceutic company, which 'selflessly' supplies also organisation-software to help ease a doctor's decision-making on medical prescriptions.

After all the commitments a medical centre demands from its doctors, it is fair in their eyes to receive appropriate compensation for their 'responsibilities' also in money-terms. Money and doctors get along with each other rather trouble free. Not many doctors can be seen to tighten their 'money-belt'. A doctor's 'nightmare' can become the following anecdote: "Two doctors have a discussion. One of them makes the statement that he has lost his 'best patient'.

The other colleague naturally asks: from what did he die? The doctor answers:

Oh no, he didn't die, he just became healthy!"

The medical centre of doctor Billy has standard business hours. Before the medical centre is closing, new arriving patients are advised to possibly see the doctors on the next day unless an emergency is coming up. Here doctor Billy steps usually in, preventing the consultation process to come to a halt as this is more likely in a one-doctor-surgery. In other words, not only 'pills' are 'pushed' in a business-like medical centre, but patients as well as money.

Also a break during the day is easier arranged as there is always somebody from the medical staff who can step in and fill such a gap. All in all it does appear that "pill-pushers' have a 'better'life than the 'family-doctors' of the past. How would this compare with quality of help, in which the human 'factor' undoubtedly is equally important?

Judging humans and their behaviour is not only a matter of experience, it is also said to be an art. Doctors have to rely heavily on such a knowledge of human behaviour, when they want to reach a true balanced diagnosis.

The 'human factor' cannot be neglected, regardless of a technological progress also in medicine. The question is now, who can serve better the said 'human factor'?

A 'family-doctor' or a business structured modern 'medical-centre' with its 'pill-pushers'? Generally speaking, it is neither an answer in 'black' nor 'white'. When medical practitioners aim for one and the same 'human-factor', the more modern 'medical-centre' establishments will confirm that modern medicine has left less room for 'human-considerations' in a growing demand for economical justifications.

And if a high degree of such 'human considerations' is maintained, it will register knowingly or not with our modern 'stress'. 'Stress' is an outcome of something we cannot manage as a whole.

Also modern progress doesn't come without a price, and one price to pay has become stress. Here is the 'come-' comedian-conclusion' for the 'pill-pushers': a quick 'pill-push' can leave the 'pill-pusher' vulnerable to the comedian of stress.

Doctor Billy's working day comes surely to an end, too. After-hour patient visits are covered in turns by all three doctors of the medical centre. And when it is not Billy's turn, he is the lucky one to see his home and family earlier for a change. This leaves for a doctor more possibilities open to have time off after work. The choice is here also for a doctor to keep his leisure time in check, so that the next day can again be committed to work.

PILL-PUSHER- CONCLUSION

If something hasn't been said yet, here is the summary trying to close a gap in a 'final stamp of approval'. It is the author's utmost desire that any reader can enjoy the look into another 'mirror' even if one dis-covers his own 'picture'. A search for truth in a comedy is not secure from controversy either. Controversies are not here to derail good intentions, otherwise we could never have a last laugh. It is also good to remember that 'he who laughs, lives longest' and the author wishes the reader only to live longest.

How far has this comedy cast light on the doctor who unofficially cops from patients mainly the 'honour' of a 'pill-pusher'? The best answer to a challenge also for a doctor, specially in a comedy, is to accept the challenge of a 'pill-pusher' with distinction. And how is that done? Make sure that the name is turned into an honourable one through distinct actions and not only words. A doctor on the centre-stage in a 'comedy' decides for himself where he stands. One secret is: as it is generally known, "a name is only 'sound' and 'smoke' ". Every name receives the significance from the 'owner' of a name or title.

As I write this comedy, population is said to have passed globally the seven billion. This growth of human beings on earth enforces also changes in the way societies have lived and live to date. One of these many changes has taken place in a health service shifting away from the 'family-doctor' to a service that can handle bigger numbers of patients.

A result has become the 'pill-pusher'. In a 'doctor-jungle' of today it is up to every individual who seeks medical help to find the 'family-doctor' from the past who can serve a patient's needs best. The family-doctors are still around amongst so many other doctors. They need to only be recognised in a doctors' 'sheep-herd'. Quality of services is also here likely to become more the 'comedian' of a quantity that has to be served.

3.) 'MOUTH – PLUMBER'

What has a "mouth-plumber" to do here with medical doctors, 'comedian' or not? Certainly a more commonly accepted name would be that of the 'dentist'. 'Mouth-plumber' or 'dentist', both do the work in people's mouths where teeth have their 'home'. No matter how many teeth call a mouth home, work on them is guaranteed the more has been done.

What is the name of a 'plumber' doing here? Unofficially the public is mainly using the name of a "mouth-plumber" for a dentist. A little of both can be found in this nick-name: as well a joke as facts. Why this is so, let's find out about it.

It is also an open secret that medical doctors consider being in a class of their own when it comes to sharing professional views on one and the same eye-level: fixing teeth is 'plumbing-work' always asking to return for more work like leaking pipes. To be honest, 'mouth-plumbers', alias 'dentists', are certainly serious enough going after their business like everybody else does. They also know how the dollar makes their work worthwhile. So, how would a dentist's working day look like?

On weekday-mornings there is no rush for Ken to go after his dental-surgery business. We 'come to the party' and call his work-place as he would like it, a dental surgery. At home his kids are the first ones to get out of their beds. The kids invite Ken's wife unmistakably noisy to start the day. Any time before seven o'clock in the morning, Ken would pull the blanket over his head trying hard to catch up with some more sleep. Just when the kids get ready to leave for school, Ken gets out of the bed, too. A quick morning-welcome ensures that the family sees each other before everybody is heading into a different direction. Until Ken gets ready for his day, his wife gives the kids a lift to the school with the family car. On her return, they still have enough time to share a cup a coffee.

Ken's wife helps on the administration side of the dental surgery, which is located in the town's centre. She is not working full-time. She keeps also an eye on the medical staff working with her husband. It is she who makes the decision about the staff recruitment in order to keep the surgery purely professional. She stands with both legs on firm ground knowing too well that a close working-proximity with an attractive patient or assistant can divert from the professional attention.

Ken's dental surgery is a modern set-up, modern technology included. Many years back when technology was still in its cradle, a dentist's work consisted mainly of pulling bad teeth out to one's best ability. Nowadays, technology has invaded also the dental-surgery.

Countless gadgets, little 'miracle' pastes and pills help to keep teeth in a patient's mouth. For the sake of progress, short-cuts are often made even at an early age and remove all natural teeth and replace them with 'good looking' false teeth. 'Good look' is a part of 'fashion', which asks always for a price to pay, not only in dollar-terms but also in comfort.

Ken's dental surgery takes into consideration the constant increasing number of patients seeking dental treatment. Bad eating habits and 'fast-food', successfully promoted through advertisements, are also feeding increasing patient-numbers to the dentist. The answer of Ken to this problem is to streamline a patient-influx into his dental surgery. Let's have a look how he has done it: Not one but six treatment-rooms are located next to each other along a corridor. Six patients are treated continuously at a time. To make sure, treatment steps are not mixed up between patients, a computer screen in each room documents the steps.

One assistant is always with the doctor, while two other keep an eye on the other patients during the treatment. The reception is attended in between by one of the assistants. Here in the dental-surgery not the patient is on a 'conveyer belt' but the dentist and his assistants, too.

Six patients are usually 'turned over' within half an hour in the six rooms. During the day this amounts up to one hundred patients, which is regarded in dental-terms a 'good daily business', usually starting in the first room: "Open your mouth = five dollars please, say 'ah' and keep your tongue back = five dollars please, where is the problem and what was done last time = five dollars please. Do you feel anything?" "It's hurting here." "Show it with your finger = five dollars please." – "Rinse your mouth and close again = five dollars please, now open the mouth again and keep open = five dollars please.

Here we are. We prepare today the tooth-filling = five dollars please.

You have better a needle for your own com-fort = ten dollars please." To the assistant: "Get the necessary preparation on the way while I see the next patient."

This 'standard dentist-procedure' with standard fees applies to every patient. The understanding of this 'mouth-plumber' is that every patient receives the individual necessary treatment, at individual prices of course.

He moves on to the next patient.

"How have you been? Any more pain?" – "Still a little bit" – "This is nothing, after today your tooth will be finished and we have to see you again first in two weeks. I take now out the provisional filling and my assistant prepares the final one. To keep you comfortable, I better give you a little anaesthetic with the needle. I'll be back shortly.

The next patient is unfortunate, because the severe pain indicates to the doctor that the tooth cannot be saved. "You should have seen me much earlier and I could have saved your tooth, now we've got no other option but pull it out. Assistant, please, get everything ready for this procedure. After I've seen the next patient, I'll return and release our patient from his pain.

In the room number four: "Has the pain gone after the last treatment?"

"Not at night, when I want to sleep."

"We certainly can help it, I do a bit more today and we are going to watch it until next time."

Back in room number three: "Is the needle already working? Does the area feel numb?" – "Yes it does."

"So we are ready, I do my best to make it quick. Here it is, it was a hard one, this pad will stop the bleeding and this tooth won't give you trouble any more. A new tooth will nicely fill this gap. See us in a month time to discuss this procedure. For only a little cash your look can be restored to its former glory."

The patient cannot first talk properly after the tooth extraction, thinking however by himself: "What would a little cash be for a dentist? I better ask now."

"Did you say 'little'? What would it be?"

"Four thousand dollars will do the whole job" responds the mouth-plumber-dentist'.

"I've now even more trouble to speak properly but I need to let you know that your idea of 'little' is not so 'little' at all. I'm earning this sort of money in one month. Since when is a tooth worth so much?" – "You can make up your mind which way you want to go. I've to do a job, see you again in a month."

Next on the line, room number five: "What can I see, a familiar face for a change! How have you been since I last saw you?"

"I don't know what it is, when I see you, the dentist, my tooth-ache is suddenly gone. I bet, when I leave here, it will haunt me again."

"We have heard this before, I can help you with that. Open your mouth. Tell me when you feel this knock on your teeth." – "Au! That's it! The pain is back! Don't do any more, please!"

"We make an x-ray of the area. It will tell us what is wrong. It looks like we've to make a couple of appointments for that. In a few minutes we'll know more."

Patient number six is not far. "What can I do for you? Where is the shoe pinching?"

"When you ask for my shoe, there is nothing wrong. My mouth however is terribly swollen, I don't know where it comes from."

"There is almost nothing we can't fix. Have you been sick lately with a flu?" – "Not that I know!"

"We first put an ice-pack onto your cheek which should help that you can open your mouth for an inspection."

The first round is over. Ken goes back to the first room to follow up what has been established. With the help of his three assistants all the rounds from patient one to patient six are straight forward and on time.

Drilling, filling, scraping, polishing, occasionally pulling out a tooth, this and much more make up for a 'mouth-plumber's' work. Intensive light sources direct daylight into patient-mouths while they are bound in comfort on a 'dental-bed'. The eyes of a patient are looking at the ceiling where they can find peace and quiet on a dense, lush green forest image. It is put in place to divert a patient's attention from the high resonating noise of the dentist's drill and cut partly out the white clinical uniforms of a dental-personnel. Light background music can eventually help ease patient-tension during dental procedures. Dentists know quite well that some patients have already nightmares ahead of their visit to a dentist.

It is important for both, the patient and dentist, to meet on common ground, so that especially the patient can be confident enough and comes back to further appointments. A patient needs the dentist to receive dental help, while the dentist can do nothing without patients. This dependence creates for the dentist his comedian-situation. To like a dentist, is for a patient almost as important as the dental treatment. A direct result out of it is, whether money comes into a 'mouth-plumber's' business or not. All eyes are on a patient's satisfaction.

At Ken's 'mouth-plumber business', satisfaction culminates with a delicious sweet, which is offered in the reception to patients on their last visit. It is a gentle reminder to come and see the dentist again. The sweet might however work in two ways, not only as a reminder but also supporting dental caries if teeth are not cleaned soon after. The 'mouth-plumber' will most likely be still around to fix also a new problem.

The day in the dental surgery moves ahead to plan. Enough patients have visited in turns the six 'treatment-stations'. At the end of the day the target of one hundred patients has been reached, so that the remaining half an Hour before six p.m. allows the scaling down of the operation in Ken's dental surgery. Ken grabs the opportunity and for a change calls it an early day. On his way out, he tells his staff: "It has been my pleasure to work today with all of you. I leave the place in your capable hands. Make sure, the place is properly closed down when you leave. See you again tomorrow."

At home the children welcome their dad with open arms: "Can we go to the movies tonight since you returned much earlier from work?" - Dad answers: "Have you done your homework, been good kids and behaved yourselves?" – "Mum, can we go to the movies?" – "Of course you can, when you have tidied up your rooms, but not before I've inspected them."- "Can we go with the kids from next door and you pick us up again?" – "I go and talk to the neighbours and see what we can do. Meanwhile behave yourselves and do what you are told." - When she returns from the neighbours, the kids are already busy cleaning up the mess in their rooms putting everything back more or less into order.

"Ken, we have the evening for us without the kids! Think of something what we could do."

The rest of the day passes anything but quicker than the working hours in the surgery. A good night's sleep is then all a dentist-family needs for another day to start well.

MOUTH-PLUMBER- CONCLUSION

Did the 'comedy' succeed also here to banish the 'comedian' from taking over a dentist's day? When the name of a "mouth-plumber" has been turned into an honourable one, nothing is left to complain and every-thing is all smiles. If controversy is an issue, it can 'hold water' only with a controversial person. Such is the rule of a comedy: if you can't laugh, just leave it!

Now, how much have we learnt about the "mouth-plumber", alias 'dentist'? In the medical family the dentists are a class of their own. The author can recall when attending lectures in anatomy at the university, a

professor speaking out on dental work: "Any intervention going past the tooth's enamel, should not be allowed, much of the dentist's work is bodged." What does the person think haunted by a real tooth ache:

"Theory wouldn't help me to get rid of a terrible annoyance such as a tooth ache. I don't care what is the name of my saviour who can just give back to me normal life." Latest here comes the 'dentist-mouth-plumber' in. Dental-work finds itself in a niche of necessities, because it still proves hard to do 'mouth-plumbing-work' yourself today. For such and many other reasons, also dentists enjoy healthy 'compensation' for fiddling in other people's mouths. It is, to be honest, not everybody's preferred profession. Nobody could possibly say, he/she is a born dentist.

Incentives however are one important motor that drive societies. And as a result of that: who has seen a needy dentist? Still, a dentist can be compared with a 'dancer on the high wire', keeping in check help, need and competency. The 'comedian' is here further away as long as the 'mouth-plumber' and 'dentist' do not contradict each other, making a good name out of both.

4.) WITCH-DOCTOR

"….is a person, especially in Africa, who is believed to have special magic powers that can be used to heal people." Some of this 'hocuspocus' is today still around. When I, the author, lived and worked for a few years in South Africa, I became aware of some cults which foreign workers brought with them from other surrounding African countries. To train them in a modern industry-technology required a good measure of adaptation to their understanding in order to win them over to more modern knowledge. Some had amulets on a string or chain just disappearing on their chest under a shirt. A tiny transparent bottle, visibly filled with some liquid or a small bone-like object were typical personal companions from back home. In the nineteen-seventies the African tribes of Ovambos, Zulus, Hereros, Xosas still exercised their influence in Southern African societies. One of the African migrant-workers entrusted me one day with the secret behind his amulet. First it needs to be said that African tribes take their cultural expressions very seriously. Under no circumstances will they tolerate inappropriate inquisitiveness. In my office I was told confidentially about the existence of his amulet-necklace: "The 'witch-doctor' or 'medicine-man' as he is called in Southern Africa, gave me it on my farewell to accompany me while I am away from my larger tribe-family. I'm not allowed to lose it and if this would happen, I cannot go back any more to my family and tribe. The medicine-man would not accept me, because I lost his protection. It would be a serious matter, depending on how the medicine-man sees my case. Sometimes significant presents brought along have changed his mind about a banishment or severe punishment. The great medicine-man is powerful, his power is in that bottle. I'm supposed not to show it to people outside my tribe. Please, don't tell anybody what I told you."

Now forty years later, I believe, I can talk about it without compromising anybody. The migrant-worker continues:

"Why I'm in the first place here, is to save money in order to buy a cow when I return to my tribe-family. I can get married only if I can afford to buy a cow. In less than a year my time will be up and I can't wait to see my future wife. I can only hope that she hasn't meanwhile married somebody else. Since you have been so good to me, I'm confident to get another work-permit, if you give me a good reference. The medicine-man will like to see it, best together with a present also from you. You should know, I belong to the Ovambo-tribe."

Time for Nguni to go back home to the far north of South West Africa, today Namibia, has arrived. The journey will take almost a week on the bus from Krugersdorp / Transvaal to his home. Reference, presents and his few belongings are all wrapped into a rug, which a strong man like Nguni just can carry into the bus. I gave him a lift and arriving at the bus-stop I couldn't believe the number of his relatives and friends who had turned up for his farewell. I thought instantly by myself:

'The bus certainly can't take all these people on board'. In front of so many onlookers, Nguni took quickly his farewell from me and left for the crowd which waited for him.

From then on not only his wrapped bundle went into the bus, but all these well-wish-presents from his own people had to go onto the bus as well. No wonder that the bus couldn't leave on time. What would an hour or so matter on a tour of one entire week. Cities were soon left behind and the true African wilder-wilderness absorbed the bus with its human cargo on semi bitumen/stony dust-roads. Also this trip came to an end. Long before the arrival of the bus at the kraal of Tsumkwe, a typical African village built with clay-huts, the message of Nguni's arrival, who also was on board, circulated already days ahead. How this happened at that time, is a real question, because the ancient messengers with their smoke-signs, were not around everywhere. So it is no wonder that the whole kraal population had turned up on the last leg of this trip. The African sun had mercilessly dried up the bush and savannah. Who lives here has to be as resilient as the African nature with its magnificent wildlife. Other rules than in a city were here established.

As soon as the bus stopped at the kraal centre-point, one woman first and then others yelled a typical welcome-call using their tongues to interrupt the call inside their mouths. Then Nguni and another two passengers emerged from the bus waving their hands over their heads.

The drum-man took over signalling throughout the kraal that 'a prodigal son' has come home. One family member immediately heads for the 'medicine-man': "All mighty 'Shaman', our son is back and wants to pay his respects to you. When do you like to see him?" "Ah, this is a good omen, when 'lost sons' return where they belong to. I want to see him right now and see for myself, if he has changed and whether he is still worthy of living with us in the kraal. Go and make sure he sees me first."

Nguni set off to see the medicine-man straight away even before seeing his kinship. He knew too well that the medicine-man determines the course of his return. The medicine-man awaited him outside his hut, sitting on a three legged chair covered with a leopard-skin. Nguin stopped in front of the medicine-man, his eyes firmly on the ground saying nothing.

"Nguni you are a good son, because you have returned to your origins. Have you also been good and respected our life while away in this other world? May our 'Good Ghosts' forgive you for going so far away."

"Thanks 'Mighty Shaman' for your goodness. To show you that I've not forgotten you, here is my present for you. I hope, you will like it. It came all the way with me." – "What is it? What is it doing? Tell me, so that I can tell you whether I like it or not." - "Do you want me to open it for you?" – "Go ahead and don't make it too exciting!" – "This small wooden box you can open here on the front. Watch what comes out. Here it is! Isn't this fairy-princess beautiful and how she can sing?" – "Don't keep talking, I want to listen to her song." – "And when the melody comes to an end, the princess returns into the box while you close its top again. Once you open the box again, the princess sings her melody again for you." - "Let me try it. The box is closed now, indeed the princess disappeared. Now I open the box and she sings again for me. Fantastic, you can go now, leave it with me. I'll catch with you later up."

A child has remained in every adult, and the medicine-man is no exemption. The home-coming Nguni is a clever young man, who didn't lose touch with his own people in the kraal, still knowing how to please specially the medicine-man.

Nguni turned to his next-of-kin to whom he had brought a little present each, too. This was a good way to buy his freedom back at home and avoid too personal questions at least in the beginning.

However, as soon as the first joy dissipated, the medicine-man was the one, who wanted to see Nguni again. "How have you been, away on foreign soil? Our 'Good Ghosts' must have protected you. Have you been sick and the other 'Magicians' had a go at you?" – "Your power has protected me well from sickness while I was in this other world of so many traps, called 'the modern world'." – "That's fair dinkum. Have you also remained faithful to your kinship and tribe? Not engaged to another woman? Your fiancée has been waiting for you trustfully."

"I've saved also some money and will go tomorrow to the market in our neighbourhood to buy a cow, so that I can ask my fiancée's family to prepare our wedding in three months, if your 'Greatness' can give the seal of approval." – "Don't rush things, you were not yet with us a few hours earlier. Everything needs its own time. I better consult our mighty nature and its messengers whether they favour your plans or not. I'm still going to pray to our 'Good Ghosts' today. Tomorrow I'll look also at your health. Somebody who has been away so far and long, could bring misfortune with hidden 'bad ghosts' to our people."

Ceremonial assistants, within the kraal, close to the medicine-man are still called in later during the afternoon. A strong bitter-sweet smell fills the air around a fire with a pot cooking cacti for a drink. Three ceremonial assistants have turned up. Everybody holds in his hands a wooden bowl with the magic drink, waiting for it to cool down in the fresh breeze that falls down from the surrounding hills during dusk-hours.

The medicine-man opened the ceremony: "We've come together to consult our all-mighty ghost-world about our latest event in our kraal. Nguni has come home, will also the good omens be with him? You have to kill this chook now and show me its intestines which will reveal approval or disapproval for our request.

First a sip from our cups and you do as you are told. Make a clean offering."

Then the medicine-man continues:

"Aba-ka-babra, Ghosts all-mighty, who is right, who is wrong? Most of the intestines look healthy and straight, therefore we are right. – Now let's see what bird is still in the sky, telling us what the near future holds.

Before that, we have another sip out of our bowl which helps to open our minds. - The Blue-Cranes fly east where the sun will rise again in the morning. Our near future is therefore looking bright. We can't have any better news. The rest of the evening can be spent finishing our drink and everybody who can add a story to this fortunate outcome, is also welcome."

Next morning, Nguni was called again to see the medicine-man: "You are fortunate, all signs were good yesterday. What remains, is to check your health as I already mentioned to you. How do you feel?"

"Quite good to be back at home".

"Did you take any 'hocus-pocus-medicine' from those new-world-doctors? I need to know about it, because my medicine doesn't get along with those other healing practices. Your amulet-bottle tells me that my medicine has been better than this modern medicine."

"I haven't been sick, because I wanted to come back to my tribe. I might consider later to work again in the south to help establish my future family better." – "Take it easy! You've just arrived and can't talk already about leaving. What do you reckon your family and friends think of you when they hear this? Better forget about what you just said and be proud of our way of life. Who will come to your rescue in case bad luck hits you in this other strange world? Rather stay with us, because we look after each other.

Anyway, I return to your health-issue. Drink tonight this cocktail before going to bed. It will clean out tomorrow all the bad stuff you collected while you were away. As a sign of your obedience, we smoke together my peace-pipe. You should smoke first in order to prove that you are a man now who can lead a family into the future. I'll let everybody know this. Any problems, remember that's what I'm here for. With our people, you are never alone. My eyes are everywhere and I see everything, that's why I can always help. We all got in us as well the bad as good ghosts. My vision and beliefs keep the bad ghosts in check, but only if people haven't a wrong mind of their own. Experience is what matters, and your medicine-man or witch-doctor, as the other people call me, has the power through life-experiences. I don't want to be called a 'doctor', because my wisdom to help and heal is so much older than all this modern stuff of today. It dates back to more than any humans can remember, thousands of years, and is only handed down from generation to generation by our exemplary tradition. Don't turn disloyal to your traditional Ovambo-roots. We have survived longer than this modern 'mop'. - I've said enough to welcome you back into our fold. If you don't come to see me regularly, I make sure this is going to happen."

WITCH-DOCTOR- CONCLUSION

Where is here the 'comedian' of the 'witch-doctor'? When comparing the 'medical doctor' with the 'witch-doctor' or 'medicine-man', there is little comparison. A 'medical doctor' lives more in the present while the 'witch-doctor' traces back a tradition to a long forgotten past. What might speak for the 'witch doctor', is his centre-position with his people. From his people the 'witch doctor' also receives confirmation of his position.

The comedian can change 'camp' here. At one time the witch doctor is the 'comedian' of ghosts and tradition until he receives confirmation from his followers. Then the 'comedian' is passed onto the people worshipping a 'witch-doctor' or medicine-man. Only if the 'medicine-man' raises doubts and cannot succeed with his title and power, the 'comedian' is more likely to remain with him. A bit of this is alive with both, a medical- as well as witch-doctor. People have rather high expectations for any doctors and don't want to see a short-fall. The position given to them in societies is seen by the public as an obligation. Doctors taking this into account, operate in the cases of a 'medical-' and 'witch-doctor' from different backgrounds: the 'medical-doctor' relates to knowledge, whereas the 'witch-doctor' to the unknown.

In the end they both draw power from people's ignorance. And it's no secret that this is one recipe how to gain power or at the least enjoy esteem.

5.) SURGEON

Does a surgeon belong to the family of medical doctors? – Yes! - Why then the name of a 'surgeon' was given to him/her?

In "Word-Origins" it is said about "surgeon": Surgeons get their name because they work with their 'hands'- that's to say, they cure people using their manual skill rather than by giving them drugs, as doctors do.

The word 'surgeon' can be traced right back to Greek 'kheir', which meant 'hand'. 'Worker with the hands' was 'kheirourgos'. This developed as it was passed on from one language to another, picking up its special medical meaning on the way, until it arrived in English as 'surgeon'.

Already in early history, a 'surgeon' was a medical professional to step out of a general medical under-standing: the 'pill-pusher' is to restore a patient's health. When this couldn't deliver any more convincingly, the surgeon stepped in with inquisitiveness first in order to find out more what is behind an illness and get to the bottom of problems. The wish to find out, is an old human aspiration. Since 'Hippocrates', 500 B.C. a treatment principle was: Where there is pus, it must be opened – (In Latin: 'ubi pus, ibi evacu)

Even much earlier, the 'Incas' and Egyptians opened the human 'cranium' (skull), favourably an enemy-one, as a cultural ritual, to simply 'find out what was behind it'.

As religion forbade to unravel 'God's Creations' no matter by what means, early surgery took hold with vagrant 'tooth-breakers', 'stone-masons' and 'artists'. No wonder that the reputation of this early 'surgical craftsmanship' was not highly regarded. A status-difference between a doctor and a surgeon was abolished in Prussia first in 1852, when surgeon-studies were established as specialised ones at a university. Before that time, surgery remained controversial. In other words, a more open 'comedian-territory'.

Leonardo Da Vinci, an Italian artist, sculptor, architect, natural scientist and technician, who lived from 1452 to 1519, became the first known person escaping capital punishment enforced by the Catholic Clergy because of secret autopsy-proceedings. Many others who dabbled in surgical proceedings, suffered until then and after the fate of capital punishment. Only self-accusation and influential personal contacts saved at the time Leonardo Da Vinci from a death-row.

Now, how would a surgeon's daily life look today in the twenty-first century? And where is here the 'comedian' that has to be taken also into account? After a small window into the history of initial controversy between doctors and surgeons, a surgeon can be sure to have an undisputed respect in the wider community. One division however has still remained, namely that of the internist versus the surgeon. The internist is the one advising a patient with the options of a healing process away from the surgeon's 'scalpel'. Synthetic- as well as natural medicines including therapeutic measures like diet, exercise, change of living habits are the 'weapons' of doctors in the 'internist-branch'. The surgeon on the other hand is trying to get to the roots of a health problem and eradicate it by cutting out the 'bad' or replace it with something 'good'.

Surgeons are busy people, because in our progressing societies sickness is increasing. In many cases, the 'knife' or 'scalpel' as it is known by medical professionals, is the last and only option to help a patient.

Surgeon Peter is doing shift-work in a major hospital. It's already here that the 'comedian' comes in. Shift-work is known to offset the 'body-clock' which nature has tuned in with the changing day and night.

Peter is doing his best to cover work-requirements and those of his family. This week Peter has the night-shift starting ten o'clock p.m. and finishing six o'clock a.m. He looks at his working hours from a positive angle: "Humans too are driven by habits, it's only a matter of time to get there." It is the view of Peter although he knows quite well that health is an issue here.

The positive side of that day is, he can see his three children in the morning before the mother brings them to school with her own car. In the afternoon it is more or less the same. The children are back again with mum, so that the whole family can spend some time together.

During the day Peter's wife keeps quiet not to disturb his day-sleep. Peter gets often up at the arrival of the children. Shopping, a visit, pursuing one of his many hobbies, all has to fit into the few hours before the surgeon's duty is calling again at the hospital.

It has to happen without excuses, because the surgeon on duty also wants to call his day and not wait for the shift-change. Sometimes this can become a problem and a shift is extended until relief turns up.

Those are days better not to be remembered. Surgery doesn't always stop as planned, which requires extra time of a surgery-team. For a good reason, surgeons do not take over other colleagues work, only in emergencies.

Today is a normal day for Peter. He arrives half an hour earlier at the hospital in order to discuss and prepare with his team the start of the shift. Patient-records are examined and previous surgery is especially followed up with an eventual visit to the intensive-care unit. Just when the preparations are on the way for a minor surgery, the emergency department delivers a case of great concern. Also here is the rule, a more serious case has priority.

Peter has seen in his twenty years as a surgeon all kind of clinical emergencies, but not yet one like this. A poor elderly man was apparently walking to his hobby-garden pulling his cart, when a reckless car driver hit him from behind. The image of what happened is too distressing to tell. Even Peter could hardly believe that the man was still alive. It was now the highest emergency. Calm remains the order of every minute in an operating theatre. Peter calls a colleague to discuss first procedures. It has taken Peter and his team not only the whole shift to patch up the almost impossible, but long extra hours from which no surgeon could walk away. These long intense hours left their marks visibly wet on the back of every-body's protective clothing. In the end, the patient survived and this was the greatest relief for everybody in Peter's team. The intensive-care-unit and nurses will continue to build on the patient's recovery. How far can success be achieved here, considering the serious circumstances the patient was in, is in the hands of 'higher authorities'.

Surgery has given life another chance. All what remains, is the hope for a better to continue.

Each team-member had a cup of coffee in Peter's office. "Not what a day, but what a night!" were the first words Peter could say. He continued: "I thank everybody for the valuable assistance last night. This is enough, let's all go home and have a rest, so that tomorrow can be another day, hopefully not a repeat. Let me also tomorrow know, who wants to have the extra time paid or extra time off. I leave it with you. I want everybody out here now, others have taken already over.

Thanks again, and see you tomorrow 'all in one piece'."

At home the wife has already been used Peter coming home at irregular times. She also knows that it is no use to call a surgeon at work. It was not only the hours making Peter tired but more so the concentration required during surgery where a patient's life was hanging on the thinnest possible thread. When everything goes to plan, a positive outcome cannot completely outweigh a tension build-up during difficult surgery.

Even before going back home, Peter visits the town's indoor swimming pool. He knows too well that swim-ming is a good, natural way to recover from stress. When arriving at home, everything is almost back to normal so that his family can enjoy a carefree husband and father alike. Specially the children help Peter take his mind off surgeon's work. Their expectations and way of thinking are so much simpler than adults have been used to in an unforgiving competitive crazy world. It's no doubt, good to wind back to something more simple after a shift-work, especially for a surgeon: one by one, every of his children tells Peter about the day at school. Despite an advanced afternoon hour, he takes his time for his family, which is another way for Peter to recover from a strained shift-work. A short, good sleep is in his eyes better than a sleep with worries. Peter tells his wife about the shift-events later, first after the children have turned their attention to some necessary home-work. He doesn't want them to pick up worries too early in their lives. Life won't spare them these experiences anyway.

It's usually his wife, who is asking how work was, when they are amongst themselves. The wife's support had been also in the past a valuable personal assistance in the daily demands on a surgeon. Not only once, but every so often Peter came home visibly down from a day's events. His wife senses already by her husband's mood, when he steps through the house door, how the shift was.

No word, she knows, problems are still haunting Peter. She usually waits to let the work-pressure come down in their cosy home-atmosphere. Occasionally it happens however that Peter can't hold back and bursts out with something like: "I don't know whether I can take more of this." The wife is then quick to respond: "Don't let problems get on top of you. Tomorrow will be another day and everything will look brighter again after a good relaxing rest. Have a shower first and after the kids have settled early enough, you tell me where the shoe still pinches. You know, I'm always here for you."

"Thanks God, I have a wife who understands me so well. It must have been the never failing love to bring us closer. Already talking can make a big difference. When people stop talking, all is lost."

When Peter keeps quiet coming home, she still takes the initiative diverting the attention away from work for instance like this:

"It' so nice that you have come today just in time to witness how beautifully our daughter plays the piano. John, you too get ready and play something for dad on your violin. I'll get an ice-cream ready for the audience while Susan prepares herself with her latest piano-piece. I declare the concert open. John please take a seat with us and after Susan has played, we also listen to you.- Susan, please tell us the name of your piece, the composer and everything else you can add to its introduction. If one day you want to become a piano virtuoso, you can't start learning to present yourself, early enough." – "I am Susan and I'd like to play for you, Vienna Sonatine Number One, C-major, by Wolfgang Amadeus Mozart, Koechel Register 439b, in 1783."

Music is the easiest language to understand. It can take our minds into unexpected fields, which include to gain distance as well from our 'blinkers-in-deadlock' as unleash surprising healing forces. The applause for Susan's piano performance just does this. Peter is already a world away from where he was only an hour ago. John just continues to do the same with his violin performance of: "Andante Con Variazoni" by Joseph Haydn.

It's hard to believe what 'expert-diplomacy' of Peter's wife has achieved. No worries, no headaches in the family any more. What appeared to be problems, the own music in particular has helped to retreat. A vernacular also says: where there is a successful man, a woman has always been close by. And no doubt, a good surgeon has to be a successful man, too.

SURGEON- CONCLUSION

As outlined, the former disputed surgeon has been reinstated in the medical ranks quite a while ago. His manual skills moved him especially with modern technological progress into specialist-rankings. The 'back-then-comedian' climbed up the ladder to a special recognition.

A today's surgeon is a medical doctor anyway, but has additional years of surgical-studies which include on the job-training. The 'comedian' has nevertheless remained his constant undercover-companion, at least unofficially.

The higher a ranking and expectations are in societies, the more sophisticated the 'comedians' follow a daily life. Here in the case of a surgeon, stress can become a daily occurrence when circumstances other than the own ones take a foothold: long working hours, difficult employee relations, personal or family-problems feeding back into work performance, losing touch with some basics like dealing with one thing at a time and building consequently on it, or simply forgetting how to gain acceptance in an eventually self-inflicted lonely position from other fellow-humans. More work in modern times is also asking for better cooperation with other people. No matter from which background people might come, exchange has become the order of the day in the widest sense.

The surgeon too is no exemption, if he/she wants to keep the 'comedians' better in check. A surgeon's day has to be different from other people's work-days, just alone because of dealings with fellow-humans in often difficult situations. Such a professional proximity to humans can empower, but also evoke controversy if the 'comedians' are not kept at bay. Also here, caution has always been the mother of wisdom.

6.) FLYING DOCTOR

Not many people have mainly outside of Australia heard of "The Flying Doctor". - Why outside of Australia? - Because it is an Australian institution. – Doctors here have gone into the air in order to service patients also outside the cities.

Let me briefly recall some of the notes I've written in my book "Road To Nitmiluk" about the "Royal Flying Doctor Service": The outback town of Cloncurry in North-Queensland is the birthplace of John Flynn, the founder of the "Royal Flying Doctor Service", a real Australian pioneering idea initiated in 1928 and still operating today across the entire 'Australian Outback'. In the 'Outback', the R.F.D.S. deserves to be mentioned mostly because of the people behind it.

Since the time of Mary Kathleen, many more courageous men and women with aircrafts have answered countless calls from people in need over an area comparable to the size of most of Europe.

Sacrifices and untold heroic actions are the legacies of this Australian institution, unique in the world. Doctors, nurses and pilots of the 'Royal Flying Doctor Service' deserve the nation's utmost respect, because they are doing more than just a job, being committed to help those in need, regardless of time, distance and whoever might be in need. A call for them has always been a serious one; no one would call because of a common cold.

There is no doubt that a "Flying Doctor" is a special doctor. Not only patients constantly change, but the challenge of distance, remote places, extreme weather conditions are always present. Additionally there is a demand of a far reaching independence in connecting to people, medical services and technical skills far away from a city-support.

Let's roll out the carpet for the 'Flying Doctor' and experience a day's work with him/her: The sun rises in a crystal clear sky, introducing another day in the far-west town of Blackall in Queensland, Australia.

"It will be another hot one!" tells the nurse the only three patients in the ward of the little outback-town. It is summer, and during the day the temperature will rise well above forty degree Celsius. Early in the day, it is still under thirty, which is a pleasant temperature for the locals.

"We'll see what the day has in store. So far we haven't received an emergency-call. But as we know, this can change quickly. Another two hours and the other nurse, Doris, will take over looking after you. Doctor Robert is due to arrive any minute." - "Good morning to everybody! Another day in our beautiful Outback-Australia. Any news, Doris?" – "Not that I know! So far it's only good news from our patients. They are just doing fine." – While doctor Robert prepares himself a cup of tea in his office, the junior-nurse rushes in with a message from the hangar where the doctor's twin-propeller aircraft is stationed: "Sir, there is an emergency in the 'Channel-Country', Fred our pilot is calling for you!"- "Thanks, I'll be straight away with him. Doris, you too, get better ready for our mission. Make sure, the patients are looked after, while we are away. I go over to see Fred right away. Don't make us waiting, please." – "Good morning Fred! What have you got for us?" "The pub in 'Kyabra' rang, a farmer is in a bad way, he just made it on his tractor to us his cut-off leg in his hands. He fell unconscious, but is still alive. Not much time is left to save him."

"Well, you know where we are heading, throw your engine on and we join you at the start of the runway. The medical equipment in the aircraft is ready to be used? I'll go and get our nurse Doris."

Four hundred fifty kilometres to the west is Kyabra, in the so-called Channel Country. Summer storms have made the dusty stone road almost impassable. The medical urgency wouldn't allow time on the road.

The best the aircraft of the Royal Doctor Flying Service can achieve, is to be there in eighty minutes from take off. No time is wasted, the seatbelts are on and a minute later the aircraft is airborne, climbing quickly up to its booked route with the airspace control centre in Longreach. By now, the sun has come up higher on the horizon. The sky is cloud-free.

Nevertheless the aircraft has to climb higher because of an unstable atmospheric layer. As soon as the aircraft has reached its height, doctor Robert asks for the pilot's additional phone: "Please, give me the number to contact the pub in Kyabra, to find out how they cope with the situation."– The connection comes on straight away: "Doctor Robert from the Royal Flying Doctor Service is already in the air, we should arrive in the next hour or so. Is the landing strip all right?" – "We had rain and the strip is muddy. Your pilot needs a good deal of experience to land here. The farmer, his name is by the way, Adam Smith, man I can tell you, he is a tough bloke, he holds his cut off leg firmly by his side as if he doesn't want to lose it. He's hanging on and we constantly stop the bleeding on his leg-wound with piles of compressed fabric. We also give him plenty to drink; I assure you, it's not whisky, but straight water."

"You are doing the right thing, just confirm that the patient is lying down flat on a bed or even a floor. Put wet cooling bandages on his forehead, neck and chest to keep wound-temperature down. Monitor his pulse and eyes. Talk to him to keep him alert. A bit of 'Coke' can in this case help, too. My contact number is ….. Any further question, please keep in touch. I'll contact you before we land anyway. You are a great help."

Turbulences from the heat-building in the air shake the plane for some time. All what this is doing, is to delay the arrival for valuable few minutes. The crew is used to different flying conditions from emergency missions over many years. The pilot is taking care of a safe passage, while its medical crew prepares itself for possible emergency procedures.

The time has arrived, the landing strip is becoming visible on the side of only a few houses in a vast country-side of bush right around to the horizon. Some ploughed farming land sticks out from the yellow, green-bush-carpet.

Fred brings the plane towards the landing strip with the wind, so that he can reduce touch-down speed to a minimum. The water and mud flies up on landing to the aircraft windows. Fred is steering the aircraft straight on the ground until it comes to a halt. Robert and Doris cannot hold their excitement back clapping their hands firmly together applauding Fred, the pilot. The aircraft door swings open and a ladder with a few steps goes onto the ground to help exit the plane. The first to get off is doctor Robert. He doesn't want to lose valuable time to see the farmer in the pub of this hamlet. Three men wait on the side of the landing strip, indicating to the doctor that he takes shoes and socks off in order to get through the mud.

Flies are the first to welcome everybody arriving here. Moving hands in front of the face can help keep these notorious flies at bay until they prove with time to be more resilient. The order was however, not to waste time with these persistent Australian Outback-creatures.

Something more important waited for the Royal Flying Doctor Service, a man's life was hanging in limbo. As soon as Doris could join Robert with the help of Fred outside the mud-area, a car waited already to take them in a hurry to the nearby pub. Doris and Robert each carried a comprehensive first-aid box. Mud on their feet was cleaned with a hose in front of the pub.

Hands received a disinfectant-cleaning and as soon as socks and shoes were back on, nothing stopped this medical team to go into the pub and find the farmer in a separate room on a bed. Robert kept his calm as usual.

First tests and procedures told him the good news: "Our fellow is still well alive despite severe shock-syndromes. First priority, is to stabilize the patient, so that we can take him on board our plane for intensive care back in the hospital. Has the pub any air conditioning unit available? The heat here is a problem. – Another thing, can you people see Fred, our pilot, and ask him what you can do to reduce the mud on the landing strip, so that we can take off again. Let's say latest in an hour."

"Leave it with us, we've got enough farming machinery around, which will push out the mud and water in order to flatten a perfect runway for you."

After intensive treatment of both, leg-stump and cut-off-leg, doctor Robert was confident, the patient will make the trip back to the hospital.

Some necessary surgical procedures were also performed. For that, doctor Robert was an experienced surgeon, too. His current acting nurse was fully trained and experienced to assist doctor Robert. Even after first medical aid had satisfactorily been completed, doctor Robert wanted no time wasted to get the patient into intensive hospital care. He was told only briefly how this incident happened: "I watched from inside the pub and realised some-thing was not right. A tractor had stopped right in front of the pub. A man was hanging strangely over the steering with his chest and head. I wasted no time to see for my-self what was going on. The two blokes in the pub joined me immediately. I was shocked when I saw the man on the tractor. He was a complete mess, actually sitting in a pool of blood. Even I must have turned 'cheese-white' when I saw a leg on the floor of the tractor. Well some-thing had to happen straight away. The two blokes helped me to carry the badly injured man into a room of my pub.

From the mess in the room you can see that we desperately tried to save the man's life. A few minutes later I called already the hospital and explained to them the emergency. Isn't it amazing, what humans sometimes can take and survive?" – "I will ask you to send a report to the hospital to my attention. Here is my business card. Please, give my nurse, Doris, some necessary details to write down. Does somebody by a chance know the name of the injured man?"

Sure, we do, he's local, his name is Adam Smith. He lives with his family on the farm where the road goes south, fifteen minutes drive from the pub." – "Can you also make sure that his family gets informed. Tell his wife that her husband will pull through. Not all is lost. - Now comes the question, how is our runway going?" – "Until you get out of here, everything will be ready for your plane to take off. Your pilot helped us to do the right thing for him." – "All I can say, typical outback-community sense, nothing is too difficult to handle. And when two good sides come together, you people and us medical ones, the 'impossible' can often be made 'possible'."

"To get you quicker out of here, my four-wheel-drive will take you with our farmer on a stretch to the aircraft without the mud-hassle. Make also sure to leave the flies here where they belong to." – "You can have them, they like us too much."

No time is wasted and the aircraft takes off without problems from the mud-drained runway. The whole farming community has come together to help clean the runway from water and mud. They didn't muck around and made a good job even in a hurry. Now some twelve tractors were lined up on the side of the runway. All the drivers and helping hands were waiting in silence wanting to pay respect to one of their own. The patient was moved on to the aircraft's own stretcher, securely strapped down, continually receiving 'bottles' under the constant supervision of Doris, the nurse. Once up in the air, doctor Robert monitors with the aircraft's medical equipment the patient's condition. – "What is the news on the weather? Will we have a smooth 'ride'?" – "Nothing out of the order, says the airspace-control-station. With the present tail-wind, we should be back quicker. How is our patient? He copped it bad.

Before we land, I'll let you know again." – "Can I have your second board-phone to inform the hospital of our arrival, so that the ambulance is already waiting for us?" - "No problem, you do what is needed. I do my best, so that we arrive as early as possible and in relative comfort."

And indeed, returning to Blackall happened fifteen minutes quicker than getting to Kyabra. The whole mission took four hours. This was only possible by air.

Without delay, farmer Adam Smith is transferred into the surgery-ward of the hospital. Fred, the pilot, takes care of the aircraft taxying it into its hangar for maintenance checks, so it is ready for another mission at any time. On the other hand, doctor Robert's mission is not over yet. The farmer and his leg has still to undergo final surgical treatment. His cut-off leg however cannot be attached any more. Too much time has passed to even consider a highly risky neurosurgical procedure. The main thing is now that everybody is happy with this outcome. The patient has made it so far through and an artificial leg can be later attached to the leg-stump, as soon as it has sufficiently healed. For further observation, the patient remains for the time being in the intensive care of the hospital. As the hospital was rather small at the time, the facilities were not exactly to the high-tech standard of much bigger hospitals in large cities. So much the more personal commitments compensate for missing high-tech components. A patient is not a number, but everybody's 'mate' living in the Australian Outback. Where humans pull together, miracles can happen like the one of the farmer, Adam Smith.

Instructions were also left with the current acting nurse to ask patient Adam about the details of his mishap, but only when he feels ready to do so. Not long after the arrival in the hospital, Adam started already asking questions: "What am I doing here? Work on the farm is waiting for me. How the hell did I end up here? The lady here looks nice. What has she got to do with me? I'm a happy man with a wife and three children.

Something must be wrong with my left leg, the way it feels under this blanket." – "Calm down, all is under control, you had a bad accident with your tractor, I was told. Can you remember what happened? Only when you feel good enough, we'd like to know also your side of the story." – "I feel not too bad, except for my bloody leg that decided to leave me. How can I do my work on the farm from now on?"

"Don't worry about that now, you are lucky to be alive. When you tell us what you can remember, we tell you in return, what we've done so far. Are you well enough to remember how this all happened?" – "Well, if I don't tell you, who else will? If I have to, I better start now: I was busy ploughing my land. I started already with day break. My 'bloody' tractor got somehow stuck because of the rain we had lately. I tell you, we can't win any more. On one side, I want the soil to be moist for ploughing, but too much wet is no good either. Well, the tractor revved its big back wheels deeper and deeper into the ground until the engine stalled. I reckon, it hit then firmer ground, but couldn't get out any more. I went off the tractor and wanted to inspect the plougher behind, whether it was ok. or not to detach it from the tractor. The moment I was between the tractor and the plougher, the 'bloody' engine of the tractor roared back into life, pulling itself out trapping me underneath the plougher. Who the hell has told the tractor to move like this? The plougher discs must have cut off my 'bloody' leg quicker than I could get out. To see my leg separated under the plougher gave me first the fright of my life. Well, feeling sorry for myself wouldn't have helped me. So I didn't muck around, grabbed the 'bloody' leg and limped on to the tractor after I pulled the shaft pin of the plougher to separate it from the tractor. For some reason, the tractor came to a halt again. It must have known that I was in urgent need of a lift. Only one thing was on my mind, to reach our hamlet of Kyabra. I must have made it but cannot remember what happened after I arrived in front of the pub. I didn't look at the mess my leg made on the tractor seat. - First now, I realise how the talking makes me weak. I leave the talking now to you and you tell me how I ended up here, in comfort I must say, while I listen." – "To keep it short not to worry you, I must say first how good and strong you've already recovered. You people must have been made out of tough material.

Anyway, I'm your nurse Doris and I was with doctor Robert and Fred the pilot of the Royal Flying Doctor Service, to pick you up in Kyabra from the pub. The pub owner and his people must have done a good job to keep you alive. After emergency treatment we straight came back and here we are."

"Does my wife know already about my stupidity?" "Please give also me your home telephone number to keep it in case we need it. I'm quite sure, the pub in Kyabra has passed on the message already."

"The wife will worry her head off when she hears what happened. I try my best to be back at home in the shortest time possible. One leg will do for the time being, this doesn't worry me too much anymore. Shit happens. The wife doesn't have to come and see me so down. She will worry less, when I am at home again."

"We'll get there slowly but surely. You better rest now."

Doctor Robert's duty for the day is so far over unless another emergency would turn up. From now on he is a free man. When Robert turns up at his home during normal daylight hours, his family values it very much. The two children ask then dad so many questions out of sheer joy that Robert is taken out of his daily routine in a matter of minutes. What matters also for him, is his family. A 'pager' which he always carries with him, plays the 'comedian-role' for the entire family. Their freedom of choice is limited by such a technical gadget. When it does ring, Robert is getting ready for the hospital, no matter where it might be. For that reason, the family plans very well for the moments they can have the beloved father. Besides a needed rest-time, hobbies like swimming, tennis,bush walking, excursions into the near-by mountain ranges partly covered with dense rainforest, taking photos, shopping, reading, practising music, working in the garden, tinkering and much more.

All this fills easily a time which is left after a flying doctor's day on duty. The emphasis is here on how to best organise the own time to fit in as much as possible. Within a busy schedule of a flying doctor, only time can mostly tell, what else really was and is possible outside a duty.

ROYAL FLYING DOCTOR SERVICE - CONCLUSION

A "Flying Doctor" is by any standards a flexible professional person. He brings his skills to 'patient-places' and not the other way around that patients come and see a doctor in an established medical place. It is partly the unknown a doctor faces when going out distances, meeting unforseen circumstances in unexpected environments. Nature as well as human unpredictability have to be taken into account to surmount controversies which could jeopardise a flying doctor's mission. Such conditions invite also a doctor's talent to improvise to the extent that unavoidable short-falls can be overcome by securing the best possible well-being of a patient. People with talents testing them in new environments, are called 'pioneers' for a good reason.

The Australian 'Outback' is an unforgiving territory, both by nature and materials. Who challenges the 'Outback' in its vastness, local people or 'imported' ones, are well advised to exercise resilience and patience.

Doctor Robert calls the 'Outback' home for a good number of years. He is known to more people than he could think of. And mainly because of his readiness to help with his expertise. The airspace has been here a challenging conquest for the Royal Flying Doctors since 1928.

Because of such diverse conditions, the 'comedian' is here diverse, too. Its profile is kept rather low, as strong personal commitments are the order. Nevertheless, the 'comedian' accompanies relentlessly also a flying doctor.

It starts with 'being on call' all day and night, making right decisions in the face of emergencies, keeping up body- and mental fitness, not to forget to also pay enough attention to the own personal life.

Many challenges can keep the 'comedian' at bay when a doctor like Robert unwaveringly accompanies those challenges with a strong personal readiness.

One worthy mentioning fact would be that the farmer incident is real and was reported also on TV in the 1990's. The location and circumstances surrounding the incident differ in this 'comedy' from the original for no other reason than to enrich the text.

CHAPTER V

PLUMBER

About 'plumbing,' there was already talk in a previous 'comedy'. Now in its very own 'comedy,' let's find out what 'plumbing' is all about. By applying the 'social ladder', a plumber can be found amongst the family of 'trades-people'.

Now just for interest, where can the 'plumber' be traced back in history? Not so long ago, water pipes used to be made of lead, simply because they could be formed easily and resisted corrosion. What took longer to find out, was the effect of lead on health. Anyway, the people who installed lead-water-pipes in homes was given the name, plumbers. It goes back to the Old French name 'plumb'and was related to the Latin 'plumbum'. 'Plumbum' means 'lead'. The person working then with 'plumbum' used to be called 'plommier' in Old French. The next step to English 'plumber' is just a logic matter of fact. How much English originates from Latin and French is shown in history, when the Normans conquered England from the Normandy in 1066 and French became the official language of the court, church and nobility. Interestingly it was also in England the 'lower classes' who resisted these changes and carried their mother-tongue through into modern times. Even today in 2018, English looks back to a seventy percent Latin- and French-origin, twenty percent German and ten percent Celtic-origin. Probably the first multi-cultural language. This is also why English can be regarded a more simple and straight forward language. After this excursion into history, let's return to today's plumber and see what 'he' has to say. 'She' is not known to have taken on a trade in the plumbing world. The exception could only prove the rule here. In other words, plumbing is predominantly a male-job.

How is a plumber making a living out of his trade? Generally speaking, a direct answer would be: not too bad at all! Some so-called 'higher educated 'ranks of society would look rather poor in comparison with the dollars most plumbers secure as an income. But then again, plumbing is also a choice of a liking in a profession. We all succeed only with what we like and not what we hate.

Tom is a local plumber in a country-town on the south-east coast of Queensland in Australia. When he was younger, he was keen to gain the various licences a plumber can have: water-, gas-, roofing- licences. Therefore he has been always busy. Those licenses differ from each other also on demands of 'working hard'. What this means, Tom can demonstrate today with a job on roof-trusses of a new house construction:

1.) ROOF-PLUMBING

Building houses doesn't stop in summer, no matter what the temperature might be. Long before the heat of a day sets in, Tom leaves home with his Ute. The wife gets up with him when it is still dark. She helps her husband to start his day at a breakfast together with no rush.

Their four children are not disturbed in their night's sleep. After Tom has left, she goes back to bed for another two hours at least. On his way to work, Tom picks up his apprentice with the Ute. The other tradesman has got his own transport. When Tom arrives at the building-site, the bricklayers are already waiting for him to finish the metal roofing sheets where the brick wall still has to go up. Roofers and bricklayers work hand in hand, because once the roofing sheets are in place, they protect the brick-work from wayward weather and of course keep the sun out.

With first daylight Tom and the apprentice are up on the roof trusses, checking the battens that all screws are in place. The instructions from the trusses to the fellow plumber on the ground: "One roofing sheet at the time. Lean it on an angle onto the gutter and secure it while we pull it up. Watch the wind, we can't have more of it, otherwise we have to stop. We rather play safe."

To the apprentice: "Watch how we put the sheet in place. A clamp goes straight away on the bottom and top, so that the wind cannot pick up the sheet. You do the bottom, I do the top. Watch your back, I don't want you fall off! You can't be a sleepy-head any more. We sleep in the bed but not on a roof. While I put the first set of roofing screws in with the battery-drill, you secure additionally the sheet in its place. We should have this roof side covered in next to no time. Finishing it off, will be another step. I shouldn't have to talk much more. We don't get paid for talking. Let's do the job before the sun burns us for too long. "

Said, and it was done. Just when the bricklayers had prepared the mortar in the mixer and allotments of bricks were close to the place where needed. The roof was provisionally in place providing a much needed shade for the bricklayers.

To the apprentice: "You see, it's not so difficult once you get the hang of it. You've done all right. Always remember, you can't sleep on the roof, it's too dangerous to fall. You on the ground, come also up, so that we can put all the screws in. You can do it while I cut the overhanging sheets and prepare the caps to go into place."

Meanwhile on the horizon the sun had risen reflecting directly the heat from the roofing sheets. The only protection against the sun in Queensland is to cut it out wherever possible. A cotton sunhat with neck protection is a must, if severe sunburn is to be prevented. People must somehow get used to these conditions, because experiencing it for the first time, gives certainly everybody a heck of a surprise. Only by doing it, one can experience this. Then probably people would also understand why the pay for this work is fairly good. It's not so much here a question of physical performance but to keep a cool head despite the often hot working conditions. Every move, every action has to be controlled, because roof-heights vary and the operations are basically the same regardless of height and heat. One mishap can become the one which is already too much.

Tom doesn't take any risks cutting short safety measures. Some other employers expect their people to work in swindling heights in order to save measures to secure roofing operations.

Even I, the author, remember having seen roof-work on twenty-five meter steel beams, where plumbers or their workers walked on the small steel faces as if on the ground. As it is however also well known, 'a jug goes to the well only as long as it breaks'.

How come that metal-roofing is part of a plumber's job? The nearest of a roof reminding of plumbing would be the rain-gutters with down-pipes. They are usually put in place first before the roofing sheets follow. Most of the time a roofing-plumber has one trade-licence just for doing work related to roofs, including drain-pipes into the ground. The advantage of Tom's other licences is that he can also do other related plumbing work: for instance, to install water tanks with pipes and pumps in order to collect rain water from the roof and in many cases to feed an household with in-house pipe-installations. This way, more of a job is under one control, which can speed up a completion considerably.

As soon as the brick-layers can continue their job under a roof, a morning break is due for Tom's plumbing-team. Now at ten am., the sun can now fry eggs on the roofing sheets. The heat can be so intense, especially in summer.

Starting early in the day is one answer, but it can't be too early first of all because of no-sufficient light and secondly, roof-trusses and metal-sheets have to be dry, in other words free of the night's dew.

Working conditions would otherwise be too slippery and consequently dangerous.

Before an afternoon storm eventually arrives, the roof is in place. Work on the roof is 'hard yakka'. The pressure to have it done before either the sun bakes people or rain spoils the work in progress, is not a child's play. So much more, skills and good workmanship can pride themselves with a job well finished. That day, a storm didn't eventuate, so that the work on the roof could be finished later in the afternoon when the sun had become less 'biting'.

During the hottest hours of the day, plumbing work inside the house was done, which is a relief operation from that on the roof. Here is one good reason why Tom had chosen to diversify his plumbing business. Tom's work-day hardly finishes on regular working hours.

His 'comedian-rule' is, work is best done as long as jobs are around. He cannot remember having difficulties to find work the last ten years.

On the contrary, work for him and his team had been and always was more than he could handle. Therefore he was in a position to carefully select jobs which suited him better. This doesn't happen overnight. Tom had to build on a sound reputation of job-quality and reliability on for many years. And he was determined to continue doing so.

Tom's wife was an accountant working side by side with him from home. She didn't not only do the accountancy but also regularly ordered the materials Tom needed. During the day when Tom was on site, they stood in contact with each other via mobile phone. This cooperation didn't work beneficial only for the plumbing business. The time at home, the wife could also dedicate to their children. All in all that means, working hand in hand gives a family time at home after a day's work.

How clever is that? One has not to be necessarily highly educated to run one's life well. Rarely after a day's work Tom's family goes after pleasure. Tom is often rather tired when he comes home and is resting first a little.

Depending on what time it is, there is usually enough time to pay attention to the children, work on his hobby-model-aircraft and do some necessary work in the house or in the garden. Dinner, TV or eventually a movie can help finish a busy day of Tom, the plumber.

The four children have an early night and when Tom and his wife finish their day, they can be sure to be tired enough to have a good night's sleep. Plumber's work is in today's business world demanding, too. It's almost like, only the mentally and physically fittest will survive.

Other interests like rugby, to spend time on the beach, go shopping, see other family members and friends, are mainly reserved for the weekend. A weekend for Tom starts on a Saturday afternoon, because plumbing work needs to be done also on Saturday mornings.

Last but not least, where has here the 'comedian-role' of a plumber been hiding? A customer is also a plumber's 'king' to whom Tom has to listen and answer. This alone doesn't make the plumber a 'comedian' but equally the job-difficulties and discomforts from varying weather conditions, hot, cold, wet, dark. So much or so little about one field of Tom's plumbing business.

2.) WATER-PLUMBING

Let's shed light into the other plumbing-field of Tom, water-plumbing-installations: It still will be the same Tom with his support-team. The difference is that on days with water-plumbing work, nobody has to get up early while it is dark. Most plumbing work is then under a roof, which keeps the sun out. Daylight is actually needed as plumbing in houses is often done before electrical work.

Tom's pick-up truck is well organised, taking into consi-deration all three plumbing fields, Tom covers. On one side are the lock-up shelves for roofing parts and materials. The opposite side holds everything Tom needs for the current water-plumbing job. And the back of the Ute-platform keeps the equipment and materials used for gas-plumbing.

A Blue-Cattle-Dog, also known as a Blue-Heeler, keeps his constant eye on the platform from the back-seat of the Ute through the rear-window. Nothing escapes his attention. Nobody else except the three of the team could take anything out of the Ute. He is quick to bark and face a stranger who would dare to take something from the Ute. He is simply the best 'mate' of the plumber's crew and everybody's best friend. A dog in the company of tradesmen is an established tradition of Australia. It is also the best, cheapest and most effective security on building sites. Any changes a dog reports straight away to his boss.

As mentioned, the day on water-plumbing-work starts usually in summer at seven in the morning and in winter at eight. Water is known to find smallest gaps to escape. This means that water could damage all the other work in a house if a plumbing job is not done properly. Also here Tom doesn't allow short-cuts. He rather does a job right, so that no claims can come back and throw his work-schedule out.

His preferred advise to house-owners is to use copper-pipes including copper-fittings. If people however do not want to go to this expenditure, he follows builders' instructions using galvanized or plastic plumbing. He makes also sure that any future problem of these choices, do not become part of his job warranty. In a competitive world there is not much room left for errors or shoddy workmanship.

On today's building site, all water-plumbing is due to get started. Pipes with their fittings, taps, shower heads, outlets, all this is put in place with a plumber's logical step by step steady approach. Considerations for an effective work are: where to start and how to proceed, get all plumbing neat and straight, fix everything without causing leaks or corrosion.

All this is an essential part of a plumber's pride. Specially the apprentice learns from the beginning of his appren-ticeship with his hands on the job that where is no joy in a job, then don't do it. And Tom tells his apprentice:

"Joy comes only when you have overcome initial problems. When problems persist, you have to try harder. Joy doesn't fall into your lap easily. We all went through this and came on top of it. Apprentice-years are no gentleman-years."

Morning tea at ten and lunch around midday are the breaks from work. Other people on the building site have to be consulted, so that no work interferes with somebody else's. For Tom this is only common sense; one can expect respect from others only the way you respect them.

Plumbing work is however not limited to areas inside buildings. Water-main to the house, sewage piping, septic systems and even lightening-conductor from the house into the ground require digging trenches on the land next to the house in order to lay the required piping. This means to work again in the sun and other weather conditions. Favourable moments without too much heat and rain come in handy for outdoor plumbing, when you have to pick and shovel soil and stones.

One secret of all work, whether hand- or brain work, is to be systematically, which means: break down a task into small manageable tasks and continue with one step at the time but not lose the end-target.

This is best done without rush, because doing things twice is the worst time-loss. Digging here can be demanding physically but is less straining when done cautiously enough. Latest when a trench for the underground pipes is not right, the one who is digging it, will experience firsthand what good organisation is all about. Only by doing something, we can really learn. An apprentice is a prime-example of learning from doing something wrong occasionally. It's no use to condemn somebody overhastily. Everybody had some-body who had the patience to give us a chance to learn from our mistakes.

The outdoor plumbing is not finished on that one day. Therefore the next day, Tom and his team start earlier to finish the job, so that the Building Inspector of the local Building Department can come to inspect the plumber's work and give his seal of approval.

Only by getting everything right, a target can be reached also in plumbing. It's usually the little things that spoil efforts and it is equally important to pay enough attention to an apprentice if he/

she is considered part of a day's toil. It's not easy to divide attention with somebody who is learning. When working with people, we can only expect what we are prepared to invest in them. Tom has enough common sense in applying the right measure to treat his staff as well correctly as necessarily firm. He too comes from the school of life.

The outcome of a day's work is always proof enough for him. Tomorrow will be another day in plumbing, too. Inspection and approval of a plumbing job is a moment of pride for everybody. On such a day, Tom thanks his work-mates and let them off 'the hook' one hour earlier than usual. A little beer on site helps then wash down some of the sweat and dust.

A day after work is not much different for Tom regardless of what kind of plumbing-work has been done. The family is again his next natural choice.

A JOB IN THE COUNTRY

A plumbing-job is never the same even regarding its location. Sometimes, Tom gets a job in the country side, mostly in a small place, because not all places have a plumber. A job becomes then a human-relation exercise, too. People in the country don't see as many people as city-folk. They are often reserved first, waiting how a 'foreigner' responds to their different life-style. A job is here never a priority, people come first. They listen carefully and want to be convinced that the right person does the job. A first meeting might sound like this: "I'm your plumber and have come today all the way from the coast. How have you been in such a nice place? Your garden looks healthy and doesn't show the drought of the last six months. You must love your garden. Is there still enough water in the ground to get pumped out?" – "Come on, look at my vegies. From the sound of it, are you country-people? Since you obviously under-stand country-life, you can find out during your breaks, how my tomatoes taste. We wait here still for the rain. How has it been on the coast?" – "The weather plays up in the place where I come from, too. Lately we have got either too much or too little of everything, never the right weather. When it rains too much, my job becomes very difficult. Anyway, we haven't got the problem of too much rain today in your place. The job should be a straight forward one. Can you show me, what you want us to do?"

"The pump with all the pipes need a good check- up. When the rain comes, I want everything to be ready to fill the water tanks and the dam next to the house, so that we don't run out of water. Have a look and when you are ready, come into the house and let my husband know, you are here. He is sick and can't come out. 'Sharpen your pencil', money doesn't grow here on trees." – "We are here to help and do our best. Do you eventually know somebody else, who requires our work here? Since we have driven almost the whole day to get us here, it would be nice to have more work in order to make our trip worthwhile." – "You just do a good job and I let my people know, you are here. This is how the country works: what comes around, goes around!"

3.) GAS-FITTING

A job-call for Tom is not necessarily only for one of these fields, water-plumbing, roofing or gas-fitting. Sometimes he gets the contract on a building site for all of them.

This works in favour of Tom, so that he has less travel-ling to do and also can work more competitively in one place. No matter what kind of plumbing is needed, the day starts and finishes for Tom and his team more or less in a similar way. Comparing a water-leak with gas-leak are however two different kettle of fish: water causes damage to a property, whereas gas can endanger lives. Gas-instal-lations are therefore subject to strict conditions. As Tom is in his team the only licence-bearer of gas-fitting, he does it all alone. His work-mates then do either something else or assist him. Gas-fitting can never be a try- and error-job. One must know what and what not to do. The legal implications for faulty work are far reaching. A plumber can end up in jail when negligence of his gas-fitting-work is proven. So far, Tom never had a problem, because he is also master of his own work and doesn't have to extend his responsibilities to somebody else. Working with equipment where gas is involved, requires also special training in welding. The worst nightmare for a plumber would be a welding job on any kind of a closed container which hadn't been effectively cleared of gas-pockets. A life-threatening explosion would be the result when welding is undertaken.

How is this dealt with? Filling a container completely with water is the answer before any kind of heat through a welding process reaches the container. This is one of the many precautions gas-fitting requires.

Here failure or negligence to safeguard knowledge is dangerous, there is no room for error. Tom is used to say: "With our job, there is no walking away from respon-sibilities with a 'golden handshake' like this happens in other so-said responsible jobs. If I don't do my job right,

I soon will have no work. Not only we, but our families will suffer, when the bread-basket is hanging higher. Instead of a 'golden handshake', I'm more likely to end up in jail." – This is also a reminder, where the 'comedian' is here hiding. At home, Tom tells his kids from time to time: "Life is not 'honey-licking'. You do your school right and you have a better chance in life. If you want something and you work for it, you deserve it. There is no such thing like getting quickly rich. And if you still see this to happen, have a look behind the scene. You'll find that not everything is gold that shines, or quickly gained is quickly gone."

Slow but sure wins the race, are good words of advice especially for the apprentice. Skills and knowledge alone won't prepare the younger generation enough for their lives. We all don't work only for the bread we earn. There is more in life what the eye cannot always see. Also plumbing-days can look like working / sleeping / working.

Plumbers have aspirations besides work, too. Tom for instance likes to go fishing with his boat. On weekends, when the weather and time allows, his whole family enjoys time on the boat. The family four wheel-drive also pulls occasionally the caravan to interesting country-sites like a waterfall on mountain slopes covered with dense rainforest. These are for Tom and his family moments to refuel energy for a working-week ahead. Compared with the working week, these special moments of a weekend are rather short. They are however incen-tives to battle the long haul during the week in order to gain the little moments of life which make it pleasant.

PLUMBER-CONCLUSION

A plumber should also be regarded belonging to a society's 'middle-class'. Everybody who earns a decent living with righteous work belongs to a so-said 'middle-class'. Hard, efficient work is here the best warrant to keep in check the 'comedian-situations' everywhere present.

Plumbing too is a professional activity worth to be looked at. It is often the ones who claim to know much, but in reality have the blinkers on in a 'glasshouse' of their own. Because they always know, they too easily miss to look outside their own territory in order to find out that there are also plumbers of which not many people know much. Only when 'necessity' catches up with 'glasshouse-inmates', they suddenly wake up and find out to their surprise: 'how expensive a plumbing job is'. And it is usually the others outside the plumbing-world to blame, because their widespread indifference towards other people's work can become such a wake-up-call. The plumber too benefits from that attitude that plumbing-work rises on the job-horizon to a well paid job with time. The more 'do-no-goods' are around, the more 'do-goods' benefit from a rising demand, here in plumbing.

CHAPTER VI

"COMEDIAN"—TEACHER

We all have teachers in our lives and also vivid recollections from the time at school and in life. Teaching doesn't start at school. The moment we are born, learning starts. And where is learning, there is more than just teachers who can teach us something. A mother, father, relatives, friends, formally appointed teachers, self-teaching, life is probably the best teacher. Above all is the nature as a teacher for those who can connect to its messages.

From early history humans have been collectors.

What has been collected stays behind when we pass away. If this is not picked up by descendants, it would be lost. Nature already demands that all creatures have descendants in order to warrant the survival of a majority-living-forms.

Since early history, humans have appointed formal teachers to collect experiences, knowledge, wisdom and pass it on not only to a younger generation but to all walks of life, too. The introduction of printed books have opened knowledge-avenues for more people. As a result the public school sprang into life during the nineteenth century. Formal, basic school-knowledge became with time compulsory. Population growth increased demand for more and diverse education. Today education covers almost all society-activity-fields. In accordance to it, teachers are also recruited from those various fields. Basically they are called: Kindergarten-Teacher, Pre-School-Teacher, Primary-School-Teacher, Secondary-School-Teacher and Tertiary Teachers.

1.) SECONDARY TEACHER

Which teachers we have mostly seen in an education? They are the Primary and Secondary Teachers. Let's therefore spin first a comedy-yarn about two teachers who earn their living in the teaching field of a Secondary School: Claudia and Colin are a teacher-couple in their forties. They look back almost twenty years of teaching at the public Secondary School of 'Georgetown' in the South East of Queensland.

Their work-day at school starts nine o'clock a.m., more comfortably than many other professions. Daughter Caroline, who is in her teens, gets up with her parents in the morning. She needs however a constant reminder. In winter it is the cold, in summer, it's something else keeping her in bed.

When the clock has failed waking her up and repeated calls from behind the door of her room couldn't get through, mother Claudia's last wake-up call is: "Get up, you lazy bones, now!" All three go then together in the family car to the not so distant school, Colin and Claudia driving in turns.

Colin and Claudia seem to have their lives well organised and yet they have even with one offspring a battle on their hands to control the daughter having her own way of life too early.

In a progressing world, everything is bound to change. And as a consequence, a price has to be paid as well. With the younger generation, teachers are in the forefront of a progressing world. Teachers are more exposed to controversies than many other professions, because also they are human beings, who err. - Years earlier, when I, the author, went to school, teachers were using strict disciplinary measures to maintain a teaching-atmosphere. To 'get a box on the ear' or the cane was that time rather humiliating for the 'receiving end' and not at all for the teacher. Most of us could still become reasonable citizens regardless of 'box on the ear' or the cane.

In a retrospective view, I must now admit, we didn't suffer from discipline.

Today, a lot has changed since my time in the nineteen-forties and fifties at school. Teachers like Claudia and Colin face today a very different school-world. The system is overriding a teacher-personality. Everything has to fit a 'majority-understanding'. The majority is here the teachers' 'comedians'. Let's find out first, how Colin and Claudia manage as teachers their school-day:

The couple, Claudia and Colin, are happy to be teachers at one and the same school. It makes their lives much easier. Instead of accommodating for two jobs in two different places, they save time and probably an extra car. Their daughter Caroline is just by a chance in a class of her mother Claudia. We look into teacher Claudia's class first.

A second school-bell rings and lessons are to begin at Georgetown-High. The door to the class-room of year ten is left open when Claudia arrives.

Inside the class is noise and turmoil. But not for much longer: "Everybody to his/her place, I speak now and you shut up! Do we understand each other? - Yes of course, we do! - That's much better! – Now we can start with our math's-lesson. Who is missing today? Are there still outstanding questions from yesterday? Don't hesitate and come forward. There is never a stupid question. You rather ask, so that I can do my best and explain once more slightly in a different way, if needed.

Take your exercise book with you to the black-board, write down what you have understood so far, so that I can explain better the rest to you.

Now you see, why the black-board is better kept clean, because you have now the 'honour' to clean it. In future don't scribble this sort of nonsense on it."

The maths-lesson of Claudia passes as planned. The one or two students who tried to disrupt the lesson with a prank, she ignored to the point: "Don't think, I miss the nonsense two students of this class instigate constantly. Every body else listens, why can't you do the same? Behave yourselves and don't become the laughing stock of your class-mates."

Sports is the other subject Claudia teaches at the school. The students who develop little interest in maths, are often the ones excelling in sports. Claudia gives here her students a chance to balance one subject with the other one. In sports she reminds for instance: "you are a good swimmer, I can't see you aren't good in maths, too. You can do it! Don't let yourself down. "

In maths on the other hand she encourages: "You are bright enough to tackle sports, you must only want it."

Teaching lessons, including the breaks, go eventually quicker for teachers than for students. A teacher is in the focus of many critical young eyes. And it doesn't stop here, teacher-colleagues, superiors, parents, the public from within and outside school, all have expectations they want teachers to live up to. Teachers are here 'the meat in the pie' and many want to have a 'slice' of it. Neither teachers can work miracles. All what it comes to, is the personal experience to stand up in the 'test-fields' of the real world.

Let's move also over to Colin and find out about his teaching. He is teaching French and Japanese. To keep discipline up in a class is a challenge of its own. Although most people would accept the fact that effective learning requires a high degree of discipline, but when it comes to apply it, public opinion differs. Again the teacher finds him-/herself in the middle of the students and parents' expectations. Colin tackles his lessons with a common sense approach: to learn a language is only natural to use it. The moment he enters a class room, he speaks the language he is teaching. Explanations are done in writing on the blackboard in very small cautious steps, for instance: 'bon jour' means 'good day', 'mes etudiants' = 'my students', 'aujoudhui nous sommes Lundi'='today we have Monday' and so forth in connection with the textbook. It is not easy to convince everybody in the class that this is the best method to learn a language. Some will try not to listen and it will be up to the teacher to win them over, so that they don't stay on the side-line. Only with time the benefit of this kind of teaching- method will become obvious. Until then, it is a teacher's battle to implement modern learning in a class. Colin is meanwhile used to deal with difficult students.

Every so often he brings his guitar to his lessons teaching his students also a song in the foreign language. This is the moment, all the students forget about any reservetions. They even copy their teacher's performance and compete in the class not only with each other but also with the teacher. It is here where Colin makes his break-through teaching a foreign language.

Colin is an advocate who stands for true-to-life teaching methods. It's like dancing on the wire: first of all, the teacher-organisation wants teachers to honour teaching-guidelines. As a matter of fact, progress cannot be stopped in education either. The difficulty is here namely, how far education authorities are prepared to go along with individual initiatives out of the practical teaching-world.

In last decades teaching has experienced major changes wittingly and unwittingly. When I, the author, go back to my school-time over sixty years ago, discipline was an undisputed 'trademark' of teachers.

During changes discipline has become the 'comedian' in today's education system. Many teachers have retreated from personal teaching-initiatives, following guidelines more from higher up. As a result, real progress is hampered in education through bureaucratic bungling.

Therefore it is so much more refreshing to find a teacher-couple like Claudia and Colin who are dedicated teachers.

Before continuing with a daily teaching of Claudia and Colin, it would be quite interesting to find out how lessons over sixty years looked like. From my own recollection, I can say that teachers were very different personalities at that time. Teachers had probably more freedom of teaching. Outside interference from parents and legislation was subordinated at school to discipline.

As discipline has become with time more and more the 'comedian', 'outside-interference' has gained the upper hand. Even back then, everything was not gold that shined nor bad. I'd like to bring from my school-time a number of 'puns' which show how teachers managed discipline in classes that time. It needs to be said before-hand: this kind of teachers' freedom should not mislead into believing that respect wasn't an issue. On the contrary, respect for teachers was undisputed.

Looking back, I got the feeling that the world was then more individually formed than it is today in the Second Millennium. With all respect, the world will continue to progress including education and teachers.

Only history will tell whether it was for the better or worse. Here are 'puns' from my school-time:

1. The English-teacher was not impressed with a student's response:

    "I strongly suggest, you could have done this much better, don't you, you 'cheeky brat'!"

2. The French teacher reminds a student: "Smith, I'm not your nanny! - What I've seen, I've seen! – You can't be right! I'll look into it at home, too. - Instead of an 'extra time' at school, I'll give you a 'Sunday-roast'.

3. The Latin teacher speaks up: "You want to be a man? Forget it! Nothing is created from nothing!

4. The maths teacher bursts out: "This class is like children! You better grow up! You are not far from a pig-sty!

5. The chemistry teacher lost his temper and had a go on a student: "I'll get you quicker than you could think and you'll get a box on your ear on top of it. Damn! This is the last straw, it breaks the camel's back! You bloody idiots! Wait until I get you! Just watch it, when I see your father or mother! "

6. Another maths teacher had a crack on students: "'Early' veggies from 'Noarden' of Morocco. - First warning! - What did you have in maths? - No wonder! – You got it! I can't see clear! The exercise needs to be 'tickled out'.

7. Even a Doctor in maths was not immune: "This asks for an invitation to the black-board, it doesn't look like you learnt it, go back to your seat, this is unacceptable.

8. The music teacher was the best. That's why he copped the nickname, 'Appendix': "Not in my lifetime I've seen such a bunch of pigs, sit down, get up, stay up. My God, is this an immature mob!

9. The sports teacher did not lag much behind the music teacher: "Boy, you better go wood-chopping. Look at my glove-size! Hallelujah, 'Amelia' figure of Christ! Go to the 'Green-Ox-Pub' in Downtown, God knows where, order yourself a beer and sausage. Show off on Sundays in your confirmation-suit. Don't however come to my gym-lessons, you 'mirror-image of a Mollycoddle'. Don't expect your sports-teacher, a father of five innocent children, to land with one foot in jail. You'll be the 'right' one to teach in the future. And the one, next to you, listen, you are excelling in Latin but in Sports you are a 'nut'.

Teachers are neither more nor less erring human beings. To compare teachers of that time with today's teachers of the Second Millennium, the difference seems to be in teachers' personal freedom.

No students were harmed by strong teacher-personalities. On the contrary, a message sank no doubt in straight away, correcting student behaviours. In some cases an approach of teachers might sound heavy-handed or even abusive. Circumstances however play also here an impor-tant role: don't take something out of its context. It should be proof enough for teachers that they did their best back then, because respect and discipline were largely problems unheard.

How does this compare with a rising liberalism in today's world? I return to the teachers, Claudia and Colin. We left Colin with his French lesson. How does he manage to get his teaching across to his students with as little as possible distraction? I'm relating here to lessons of one particular teacher during my school time. At that time it was a teacher's revolutionary approach to speak exclusively a foreign language during lessons. I can relate to Colin's French lessons mostly from there.

Colin must have experienced following similar reactions from students, including parents and his superiors: First a resistance towards the 'new', then slow acceptance sets in and when the teacher can adjust his teaching to individual needs of students, better results are all what matters in the end. One of Colin's teaching methods into his foreign language lessons is the introduction of songs accompanied by a guitar. Music is well known to be the language everybody understands.

At home, away from school, Colin and Claudia exchange often their daily teaching experiences. They also discuss the pro and cons in order to improve their teaching. As long as a teacher stands firm and can with time convince students and everybody else of his good intentions, all is well.

Teachers are in the forefront experiencing criticism, including inquisitiveness of a younger generation. Let me also mention an example of a teacher, what he did to manage a class: It needs to be said beforehand that it was a catholic school only for female students. A freshly 'baked' teacher from the university was about to start his first lesson at said school. How could it be different, when the female students turn cheeky in the beginning of a lesson. The new teacher was also good looking which only contributed to the students' challenge. The teacher waited first, standing calm behind his desk without a word. As the noise in the class didn't want to die down, the teacher tried to introduce himself with his voice raised. The class was determined not to let this teacher 'off the hook', something else had to come to the rescue: the teacher was not only teaching maths but sports, too.

With a quick thought, whether to leave this class or make the point, he stood up to this challenge: he rolled slowly both his shirt sleeves right up, bended his arms to the side and showed his flexing muscles followed by these words: "You don't want to challenge me much longer, don't you?" - An unanimously response from the 'cheeky class': "Vow!"

The ice was broken, normality returned to the teaching. The answer of the teacher was simple, special circum-stances require special measures.

Contrary to this occurrence, I also remember one teacher's dilemma to establish discipline in a class: Here the teacher sought help from the school-director, calling for outside-assistance. What the teacher didn't imme-diately realise, was that he lost his standing in the class, no matter how hard was 'clamped down' on the class with outside help. Authority has never been a result of 'clamping down' on people, rather winning over people's acceptance. This can determine very much whether a teacher's life is enjoyable or not. There are also rules in education, in order to regulate minimum demands. Any additional expectations in education can best be met with a teacher's personality.

Where this should start and end, is a question of a balance between personal commitments and talents. Discipline today has become an issue, not less important than in the past. Human Rights and personal freedom dabble also today in lessons at school.

Teachers find themselves in the middle of wishes and necessities from bureaucracy, public life and parents. It appears more convenient today to rather follow rules than allow personality to have a say in education. The question of a teacher-personality has also become the 'comedian' in a progressing society.

So much needs to be said in general in order to under-stand some of the complexities surrounding teachers.

A work-day for the teachers, Claudia and Colin, finishes at school usually a bit earlier than in the industry or many other professional fields.

Teaching the young generation is a 'different kettle of fish' all together from working with materials. Some teachers, as I can remember, worked and didn't work like a 'bricklayer' with his trowel: 'call it a day', the trowel goes. Colin and Claudia do not follow this 'bricklayer'. A dedicated teacher is found spending also some of his/her leisure time to prepare school-subjects and continue further education in a broadest sense. This is the central idea of a good teacher. There are of course also other teachers who make more or less a 'holiday' out of the time after school. These are the two options that make a dedicated or work-to-rule-teacher.

A reader of this comedy might ask: how can the author judge teachers because he is not a teacher? My answer is: experiences across many facets of life plus close observations can put you into a position to judge others more independently. Many have their views too close to their 'own mirror' and therefore the 'blinkers' on. The 'comedy' here takes better into account the views of many readers.

Once more back to a school day of Claudia and Colin: school finishes usually at three in the afternoon. Students are first to leave while teachers are engaged from time to time in other responsibilities.

Today it is Claudia's turn as a sport-teacher to dedicate an hour and a half to a community basketball-team. She enjoys motivating young people especially in sports. Benefits from sports support very much other activities as well within as outside school. While Claudia assists a community-interest in sports, Colin does some necessary shopping with his daughter together in town. Before heading home with their car, they return to the school's sport-hall to eventually watch basket- ball until it is finished. All three, Claudia, Colin and their daughter, call it together a day. Once during the week however, on a Wednesday, Colin teaches the public Japanese at the local TAFE. Not much else is left from a school day even for a teacher. Every-body making a living with work, has to find a balance between duties and leisure time. What doesn't fit into today's timetable, will eventually fit into another day.

Where is a will, there is a way. The teacher-family can do much together because of a similar timetable. Specially on school holidays, they can enjoy more leisure time than most other professions.

2.) KINDERGARTEN -TEACHER

A window into other teaching-fields helps better to understand a role, teachers play in a society. To call also this chapter a 'comedy' is simply an acknowledgement that our lives never run on an even keel.

A 'comedy' suggests therefore that we leave aside all the differences dividing us, especially through education in professions.

Let's come out of specialised professional 'glasshouses', as 'comedians' we should be able to understand each other better. How would the role of a 'comedian-teacher' look like in a Kindergarten / Preschool? The actor on centre-stage will be again a teacher.

Most of the time, the role is staged by an actress. It cannot be denied that a female-actor is placed better with young children in a 'play' than their male-counterparts. Simply, women are also the ones, who bring children into life and therefore possess by nature the necessary strength.

Again this statement allows the exemption from a rule.

Anne is the local Kindergarten-Preschool-Teacher of a small town-community. Everybody in town knows her and that she likes to work with children. No wonder, the fifteen children in her Kindergarten-Preschool like her, too. Anne herself is a mother of two children, one girl and one boy. There is no 'hanky-panky', just a husband, who gives his support.

It works well for the family that Ann has with children a part-time job. Her two own children are three and five years old. So, their mum can look after them also away from home. The husband is working in a mine. He travels to and from work daily a good number of kilometres. Back home, Anne has enough time after her duties to run the household.

Every little bit helps also this family: her income plus that of her husband, time spent with her children at home and in the Kindergarten, all this gives time back when the family is together.

A week-day starts regularly early. The husband is the first one to get up and ready for his job in the mine. Ann keeps him company until he leaves home in one of the family-cars. During work-days the children see their dad only when he returns from work, later in the afternoon.

Three days a week, Mondays, Wednesdays, Fridays, Ann works in the Kindergarten. Leaving home with her two children in the car, she gives also two other children from the neighbourhood a lift. When they arrive at their 'little-children-school', there is still some time left before the other children join at nine o'clock in the morning. All children leave their school-bags in 'pigeonholes' marked with an animal, instead of a child's name, under the veranda. They learned very quickly which animal is their 'pigeonhole'. A 'little learning' starts already here, when Ann asks daily two of the children: "Can you tell me which animal keeps an eye on your 'pigeonhole'?" - "Kangaroo is on my pigeonhole!" responds Paul. Another child, Linda, interrupts Ann: "I love my cat's purring at home. She does it especially when I get home. That's why the cat is also my pet here. I can show you the cat on my 'pigeonhole'."

"Show me and then you know where you can leave your bag.

Paul, now it's your turn to show me your kangaroo. Both of you, Linda and Paul, have done quite well. Next time two other children can tell me how they find their 'pigeonhole'."

Snacks brought along find their place in the fridge. Shoes are left orderly in a row under the veranda along the outside brick wall as well. Slippers are put on inside the school, whereas barefoot is the rule outside, in the sand and short grass.

Anne starts the day with play-time and singing. A little variety, so that the children don't lose their attention too early in the day. When the weather is fine, play-time starts in the protected yard of the school.

Often mothers of other children stay back assisting Anne in turns during the day. It is a daunting task, especially in the beginning, to have the eyes on the children all the time. After the little ones have settled in the sandpit with the colourful plastic figures and cubicles or on the slide and the older children with a ball in a separate corner, Anne makes her rounds to every child: "What do you hold in your hands. Take your duck across to the bucket, it wants to have a swim. If you dig deep enough in the sand, you might find some lost Lego's. I give you a hand to go up the slippery-slide and catch you at its end. Sandra can do it also, namely assisting the little ones. Make sure you remain on the side when you are assisting. Marc and Mickey you keep the ball, don't throw it hard, so that nobody can be hurt, learn to play by the rules, look I show you: you keep the ball while moving and pass it on only when there is somebody to catch it." - "I can throw the ball right over the pool to the other side and Mickey can catch it and returns the ball."- "I know you are good with the ball, but I still ask you not to throw it over the pool. Go on the other side, there is more space for your ball-games. You will see, it is the same fun.

We are also going shortly inside, clean your feet on the tap near the pool, get your towel from your pigeon-hole, put your slippers on first when your feet are dry. Don't rush, everything is waiting for you inside."

Inside, everybody has a drink brought from home. Ann takes care of a first group's toilet supervision. The little ones occupy small seats around a table, where a colouring book and pencils wait for each child.

The older children sit on chairs around a bigger table. They have a marble-run and a letter-puzzle in front of them. – "Aunty Ann, have you brought your guitar along today? We like to sing while you play the guitar," one child comes forward asking. – "Since you are so good kids, I didn't leave my guitar at home. Stay quiet and I go to my car to fetch the guitar." – "I can't wait to see you with the guitar. I like best singing with your guitar," another child reassures Ann.

Before anything goes further, Anne goes and grabs her guitar. On her return, all children are anxiously waiting until Ann asks: "Let's sing-along first a well-known nursery-rhyme: Twinkle, twinkle little star, how I wonder what you are …. Only after that, I introduce a new one to you, little by little."

All children like Anne, because she is always kind and patient, pays attention to every child, so that playing and learning are both enjoyable. Before boredom and tiredness set in amongst the children, a lunch break is called. Hands are washed, everything on the table is put orderly aside and the personal lunch-boxes come on instead. To keep everybody settled for lunch, Anne reads a story from a children's book.

When the lunch-break is over around half past twelve, the washing room is used to properly clean the children's teeth. Anne instructs all children how to brush their teeth efficiently: "Go with your toothbrush up and down your teeth, repeat brushing top and bottom of each mouth-side. The more you brush your teeth, however gently, the less likely you have to see a dentist too early. Rinse your glass and tooth brush, don't forget to clean the basin. Dry your mouth and face with your own towel, put it back on the rail, so that it can dry until tomorrow.

You've been good kids today so far. After your lunch-nap, as a reward you all can watch one of your favourite fairy-tale-movies an hour or so.

Next time we run our own puppet-show for a change. You remember, I play the clown and you can ask and I answer questions."

Movies is also for Anne the time to sit back and relax.

It is not the same with an own play. In both cases all the children in her Kindergarten stay quiet and behave well. After the movie-hour, children as well as Anne seem to have regained enough energy to go again out.

During this early afternoon hour, splashing in the infla-table plastic pool is often a welcome way to cool down. House-slippers are left in a dedicated place, a sun-hat goes firmly on everybody's head, good school clothes are also left in the 'pigeonholes'. Shorts and T-shirt on, towels placed on a rail-stand, nothing can hold the kids back from the little pool any more. Anne keeps her eyes on the children, so that none of them can become boisterous and spoil the fun of everybody. Some kids run around the pool splashing water, while others either sit in the shallow water or have only their legs from the side in. Anne knows already from her experience how children's joy can instantly change from calm to wild.

Almost unnoticeably she settles rebelling-children with her kindness-trademark before any quarrel takes off: "Vow, you want to copy the monster from the movie we just saw? Don't forget that the monster was a friendly one who helped everybody. You can do that, too.

I help you go to the opposite pool-side, where is more room to splash around without scaring our little ones. You are a good boy, you know that also you can earn good-behaviour-points. Do you want to lose your points today? I know, you won't."

Time in the afternoon seems to fly quicker than in the morning. In the twinkling of an eye, three o'clock in the afternoon is closing in. All children move inside but not before, after leaving sand, dirt and water outside. A final cleaning takes place in the bathroom with Anne's assistance. Every child brings his/her towel home to be exchanged for a clean one. After the school-clothes are on again, the lunch boxes and children's daily work go into the school-bags: as well colouring pages as first number- and letter-trials on paper. Some children can even add a piece of their own handicraft-work, paper-figures, plasticine- or timber-creations. Shoes from the pigeon-holes go on last and already the first parents have arrived to pick up their children. A few words are usually exchanged with Anne before a child can leave.

It ensures that only the right person picks up a child in the Kindergarten. Anne gives her two children a book to look at, or one of the many small tasks she still has to tackle after everybody else has left. The place is better put back into order before another day. Only the cleaning is daily done by a cleaner. Ann cannot leave until the cleaning is done.

Latest four o'clock in the afternoon the Kindergarten-day ends also for Ann.

Work at home doesn't go away. As soon as Ann arrives at home with her two children, she gets dinner on the way. Her husband is due to arrive from work shortly after five pm. When "Daddy is here", gets through to Anne in the kitchen, the entrance door of the house flies open and both children give their dad an enthusiastic welcome: "Dad, I can now write mum's name! Come and I show you how to do it. "The three year old daughter Alice 'bubbles out'. - "This is nothing, when you see what I can do," Brian, her five year old brother, hurries up. – "You are both very clever, give me a hand so that we bring these yummy peaches inside. You like them? Don't you?" - Inside the kitchen Barry welcomes his wife with open arms and continues: "When I saw these peaches on my way through town, I remembered you, they look almost as lovely as you. I know, you like peaches."

"I don't know about me, but the peaches look delicious and we can find out very quickly how they taste. You better wait until they are washed.- How was your day, by the way?"

"Only average, if I complained, it wouldn't help anybody. As long as I can support my lovely family, there is nothing to complain. A day at work is never the same. Sometimes a day is better, another one not so good. Today was a better one. I take it as it comes."

The family has dinner together at the table next to the kitchen. The news is also in the background of the living room on, its volume slightly turned down. After dinner, everybody helps tidy up the kitchen, so there is still time to spend together before the children go to bed. The children don't miss to remind their dad of their day's achievements:

"Daddy, come now into our rooms. See for your-self what we did in mum's place today.You must pro- mise and come to see us again in the Kindergarten. Mum is so good with everybody." – "Let me have a closer look. Indeed, this is mum's name. Who has written it?" – "Didn't I already tell you that it was me?" – "Of course you did. I'm just a bit tired to remember." - "Mum also practiced with us the nursery-rhyme,

'Twinkle, twinkle little star, how I wonder what you are'. Have you ever tried it?" – "Well, when you show me how it sounds, we should be able to sing it all together. Off we go!" – 'Twinkle, twinkle little star' sounds throughout the apartment, inviting Anne to join a happy family-singing.

Short after, Barry turns his attention to his son Brian: "You are almost a big school boy now, who is going to show me what he can do." – "Look at this aircraft which I folded from paper. Mum showed me how to do it. I throw it up into the air here and you will be surprised how well it flies." – "Show me, I can't wait! Are you going to be a pilot? When you do your school right, your dream might become true." - Off goes the folded-paper-aircraft into the room. It loses however quickly space hitting the wall. – "It was really flying outside, I promise." – "I know, the room is too small for an aircraft like this. When the weekend comes, we try it outside in the garden. What do you think?" – "Promise that you don't forget!"

Meanwhile Anne reminds: "My little darlings, it's time to go to bed. Put your rooms back in order,otherwise I can't come in and read the next chapter of 'Bunny-Rabbit'."

Alice and Brian are in a hurry to shovel everything under their beds. They almost forget to pay the bathroom a visit. – "Cheating doesn't work, you better clear away your toys and books where they belong to and I'll see first Alice in the bathroom, Brian soon after. When you kindly ask Daddy, he might give you both a hand."

Anne encourages her two children. – "Daddy, give us a hand, please! You are better than we are," Alice invites her father to join in."

"Such a nice invitation I can't resist. Look closely how it's done. I won't be for ever your nanny. Before I leave your 'territory', each of you gives me a kiss. You get my good-night-kiss in return," – the father responds.

Finally when Anne goes back for the second time into the children-rooms, she can find both children sitting right up with their back against the wall on their beds.

"What can I see? My darlings are ready for another round of reading! Ten minutes will do tonight. Next time you tidy up your rooms straight away without hiding stuff under the beds, then we'll have more time to read. Now let me see, where we stopped last night."

"I know, I can tell you. It was where the rabbit found his friend in the forest," – Alice tells her mum.

"You are dead-right, listen what the two rabbit-friends are going to do next."

Before the ten minutes reading-time is over, Anne changes over to sing her two children to fall asleep. She pulls each blanket further up, places the children's heads on the pillows, while her fingers caress their hair.

After the children are asleep, not much more time is left for Anne and Brian before they go to bed, too. To read a book, watch TV, eventually prepare something for the next day and go into Internet is the best leisure-time for Anne and Brian at the end of a week-day. Not every day is naturally the same even for this couple. Mainly weekends hold the key to more individual pastime.

3.) TERTIARY-TEACHER

Various teaching fields are not the one and only distinction of teachers. Teachers differ as to how to fulfil tasks on various education levels. Let's create also a 'window' in an all encompassing 'comedy' of 'higher education'.

A 'Professor' is widely accepted as a representative of 'higher education'. Universities are the most common institutions where professors teach. To reach such a level of competency requires also to get into a position of a professor. How does this happen? Definitely not on a fast track. A 'doctoral dissertation' and successful years of scientific research usually proceed a professorial chair at a university. Therefore it is common that professors are not widely found within a younger generation, usually first from forty years onwards. How would a 'Doctor Professor' compare with other teacher-colleagues?

Again let's roll out the 'red carpet' for a 'Doctor Professor': It depends on a society, if 'Professors' are called by their title or not. We maintain here a more modern approach and call also a 'Doctor Professor' simply by his name. The 'comedy' even calls him by his first name 'Bernard'.

Female 'Professors' are no exemption, they make a strong representation even if slightly different regarding the faculties. Nuclear-physics, engineering, medicine, astronomy, maths-science, electronics, just to name a few, are still covered by tradition predominantly by male-professors.

'Bernard', the 'comedian-professor' has a work-timetable of his own. On one hand he answers the request of the university giving lectures, while he also does scientific research on the other hand. His days start more flexible than the days in most other professions. Standard hours are allocated mainly for teaching. They do not usually amount to many hours, giving a professor enough time as well for lecture-preparations as scientific research. The standard hours which appear to be rather small, often increase considerably with research work. A 'real professor' lives for his/her scientific compassion, making him/her different from other teachers: humans aren't to a high degree centre-stage, but science more so.

Let's give this 'comedy' a start. A day for Bernard doesn't begin much different from another day. He was still working on a new project late the night before, because family-members visited him at his home.

He gives the early hour a miss, so that he could catch up with some needed night's sleep. Duties at the university make Bernard however to get out of the bed rather sooner than later. His wife and son have started already their day.

Peace and quiet have therefore gone. "When you are already busy, I can't stay back and pretend to catch up with some needed sleep. Good morning my dear wife and son. What can I see, the sun shines already into what might have yesterday been obscure, like light into a dark tunnel. Opportunities are here not to be missed. There is still enough time to inspect our pool. Eleanor, you can't refuse my invitation to start our day with a swim together." – "How could I? Our day starts already promising. It can only get better from here. Matthew, my dear son, when you leave, please make sure, the house door is closed. "

By the time they finished breakfast in the beautiful room with bay-windows on to the garden and tennis-court, the cuckoo-clock in the living room calls nine times. "I better keep moving, I don't want my students to wait. Is anything on tonight? And if so, you organise everything until I come home. I try to be back by three in the afternoon if everything goes to plan. How can I say 'to plan'? Nothing in this world is running to plan any more! - Here is a kiss for my lovely Eleanor. I hope it's not the last, because we never know. - I call you during the day. – Make also your day a good one!"

Instead of tackling the rush-traffic on the road, Bernard uses the public transport. Provided that a bus is not crowded with too many people, he can sit back, relax and spin ideas. In the morning the bus is less likely to be crowded than during the afternoon traffic-peak-hour. From the bus stop in the city it is only a few minutes walk to the medical-faculty. An entire crowd of students is also on its way into the lecture hall of the university. Many carry a brief-case with books and writing materials, fewer a case with a lap-top. The auditorium is built in a steady rising oval, so that students are not too far away from a microphone or a large blackboard covering the entire wall. Classes of any other school are signify-cantly smaller compared with the lecture-class of Professor Bernard. Students attending main medicine-lectures, like Anatomy, often run out of available seats in the auditorium.

A number of students stand during the lecture in passages. Some even turn back and organise a lecture-script from a fellow-student. Therefore it is recommended to turn up early to secure a seat in the auditorium. Ten o'clock sharp, Professor Bernard appears through a door on the side of the blackboard. The noise doesn't die down immediately, so that Professor Bernard is obliged to clearly announce his presence on the microphone: "Welcome to today's lecture! When you calm down, I can start." A few moments later, Bernard's wish has still fallen on deaf ears. Therefore he reminds once more: "I leave now and come back when it is completely silent." – And in fact, when Bernard returns, the auditorium has turned dead silent. – "This is what we need, the one who says first something, is me, nobody else. – Here are some references to today's lecture which you will need for your curriculum."

Professor Bernard faces at least two hundred fifty students in the auditorium. Students have to keep attention up in their own interest so that they don't miss any important details of the lecture. Bernard is known to be the artist who sketches in colour on the black-board anatomy-details almost as good as the best book. His lecture is made vivid, while he develops visibly his explanations incredibly fast. Some smart students can be seen taking photos for the own records from the black-board, however without flashlight. Any interference or interruption during the lecture is inappropriate. Professor Bernard allows from time to time during his lecture question-times, which are restricted not to offset the lecture program. Questions and answers not satisfactorily accomplished, can be cleared up with the professor after the lecture in his office.

Teaching at the university is by its nature more objective and therefore much less personal like teaching at schools. It has its justification in a 'higher education', in which every individual is encouraged to learn, succeed or not. It is here more about voluntary- than compulsory-learning. Students need to be motivated to reach a goal against all possible draw-backs in their studies. A Professor teaches in order to broaden knowledge in a specific field. Many of these 'building-blocks' in teaching make a comprehensive knowledge-building, which still has to meet the 'testing-fields' of a real environment.

Specially Bernard had to go a long way in order to fill the position of a Professor, because he was a prisoner of war for almost ten years. The war had only strengthened Bernard's determination to pursue his medical studies despite such a long absence from normal life. It is here, where Professor Bernard can assist students with his convincing example in a higher medical profession: "All you need is, to be determined enough pursuing your goal. Adversities on that road are companions only. Luck plays its role without doubt in everybody's life. Don't forget to give luck its chance, too. When you've been through what I've experienced, you'll know why it is so important to stay positive in order to survive. We rarely experience the worst possible scenario. There can always be worse ahead. Keep your head above water, you are young, you have the world at your feet."

Bernard's lecture of that day is split into two classes: an anatomy-lecture and anatomical dissection. The first one is to learn from the book, whereas the second one introduces specially the 'fresh' medical-student into medical reality with hands on. In the dissection-room some student-faces turn pale first before the students get eventually over a mostly unknown reality outside medical circles: coming face to face with human flesh, blood and bones. "Somebody has to do it" is the message from the autopsy-table.

A lunch-break is at midday between the two courses. An hour later students return to the dissection-room. Participation is only granted to students with a medical-pass. After another two hours, Professor Bernard is free to choose how and where he wants to spend the rest of the day. He spends usually another half an hour or so with necessary bureaucratic computer-operations. He also makes time available for students to see him.

Bernard has arranged at the university over the years to go straight home after a lecture, while he continues work on another day with research-projects in medical institutes of the university. Therefore he is one day earlier and another day later at home. Weekends are not necessarily free for Professor Bernard. Often he chooses on the weekend peace and quiet. On his own he can sometimes better progress with his research work. During the week undivided attention is hard to come by.

Now, what else can be packed into a professor's daily work? Not much else, it depends on how Bernard can organise his priorities of lectures, research, response to public demands and last but not least Bernard has also a private life. To succeed in a life as a professor, what counts is to restrict on the essentials. It is also here that Professor Bernard 'feels the comedian pinching his shoes'. Can somebody really escape from a 'comedian-role'? Much depends on an individual awareness. The intellectual strength of a professor should by all means enable him/her to pay attention to 'real-life-issues', too.

It appears therefore: the higher a position on a social ladder, the closer is the 'comedian-neighbourhood'.

What else is worth to mention about that day of Professor Bernard? Duties at the university have ended at around four in the afternoon. Today is his lucky day, so that he can head earlier home. At the university, everything can wait until next day. Nothing will really go away.

Contrary to Bernard's departure from home, late in the morning, the bus is not only late in the afternoon, but also packed with commuters. The newspaper helps him pass the time while waiting. The newspaper takes his mind off from the inconvenience when he stands packed between other people.

Bernard is not concerned, but rather content to be able to read his paper while everybody else around him tries to prevent him/herself from falling over. He is still positive to arrive at home earlier than the next day.

Finally at the doorsteps of his house, his wife Eleanor is already waiting for him: "Today, the traffic must have been heavy because you are late. Come in, I tell you my news." – "You seem excited! Your day must have been a good one. I can't wait, tell me the good news. Here is first my welcome-hug. My day was just another one at the university, not so exciting like your day probably was.

Let's take a seat in our favourite corner with the bay windows and let the setting sun shine on us." – "I've a cup of tea ready for both of us in a moment." – When they sit opposite to each other at the little, round Rococo-table, Eleanor speaks out: "Guess,who called this morning just after you left?" "You make me really curious! Family, friends? It can't be somebody else, because there are otherwise too many 'wolves in the sheep-clothing'."

"You don't like guessing, don't you? You rather want to know, my dear professor. I better let you know, otherwise we run out of time: Our niece Alice has a piano-performance in our town's beautiful baroque-hall tonight. Matthew has already organised the tickets for us three. We shouldn't miss this moment, when our family is the focus of the local attention. Alice has worked so long and hard in order to reach this level of competency. It must be in the family, don't you think so?" – "When you say so, it must be right. Actually I don't mind having this kind of distraction tonight. Music is beautiful, because we all understand and like it. There is no hard work for the audience but so much more for the musician. Half an hour should be enough to get us all ready. Perhaps I should talk only for myself, because also I know well enough that a lady needs her own time to make up her charm and beauty. Please surprise me, darling!"

A taxi was already called, so that nobody of the three had to worry about the night's traffic. At their arrival, a vibrant audience filled already the house, leaving only three seats obviously empty. Not much time is left before the piano-concert is officially opened by the head of the university's music-faculty. The piano-virtuosi dressed in an elegant colourful gown appears from behind the curtain. Eleanor can't hold back clapping her hands, inviting the whole audience to also put their hands together. What a rapturous welcome!

Bernard follows the piano-performance really relaxed. He sits right back on his soft velvet seat, sometimes closing his eyes, not to doze, but better listen to music which he would call 'from heaven'. A long and short interval divide the concert into three parts. Repeated applauses at the end only stop when the virtuosi returns to the piano and doesn't only give one 'encore' but 'encore, encore, more, more'!

After the last curtain-call, the director of the concert-hall gets onto the stage with a bunch of red carnations, handing it into the arms of the night's star, Alice. She bows low to her audience as a sign of her respect. When the applause dies down, the piano-virtuosi disappears from the side of the stage. The audience gets then up from the comfortable seats heading towards the exits which are in the back of the hall.

A few other members of the family wait in the foyer to meet with the night's heroine, Alice. As soon as everybody arrives, Bernard addresses the family: "I'd like to invite you for a glass of wine, to the restaurant around the corner. Let's give tonight's event our personal note, too. Alice, please join me, we lead the way," Bernard, the proud head of the family announces.

Another hour goes past in the blink of an eye while the wider family enjoys a rare get together.

"Tomorrow is not far any more, and a good night's sleep would be good for everybody as long as we can find our way home early enough," reminds Eleanor.

"Without our women, we could easily forget time and spend all night in front of this tasty drop of red wine. May I propose a final toast to our tonight's piano-virtuosi, our dear and lovely Alice. Keep doing what you like best! Your smile is reward enough for all of us. Cheers until another time, hopefully not in a too distant future."

The party breaks up quicker than it came together. Bernard's trio calls for two taxis, one for Alice, one for themselves. At the arrival of the first taxi, Bernard tells the driver the address of Alice, settling the fare beforehand.: "Alice, you can take this taxi with your people, our taxi is not far away. Thanks so much for your lovely evening, let's keep in touch, stay well."

Not much later, the other taxi arrives to bring the Bernard-party back home. – Bernard talks to his wife Eleanor: "Wasn't it a nice evening? Great music per-formed by our young hopeful family-member!

I don't feel tired at all. Tomorrow morning it will however be different, when the alarm clock rings. Before going to bed, I still read a bit. It won't be much longer. You can meanwhile go to bed. Please leave still the lights on for me. You'll have my good night's wish when I join you. What a long day, packed with so much interesting occurrences.

Tomorrow will be another day. I better stop thinking too far ahead, otherwise the 'sand-man' won't come to see me, too.

TEACHER-CONCLUSION

Like every other profession, Teachers are never the same like it is in every other profession.. They don't only differentiate in teaching-fields, but also in their personalities as shown here. Not many other professions are exposed to so much open scrutiny as teachers, especially from a younger, critical generation. Therefore a teacher-personality dominates above all the 'knowledge-games'.

Knowledge has always been available, a teacher-personality is however quite a different 'kettle of fish'. Personality is not a 'shelf-product' which can be obtained with money changing hands. A personality can only grow in an environment suitable for a growth. What does this mean for a teacher? The own experiences can support an understanding on the same eye-level from across different societal classes.

So is the 'comedian' kept better in check, as little or no-understanding are mainly the 'comedian-territory'.

This has been another attempt to highlight a daily milieu of different professional fields. The more we know about each other, the more barriers can eventually come down, which shows that we are not so much different at all. The differences are the hiding-places for our 'comedians'. And to get the 'comedian' out of the hiding-places, a helping hand can be the 'funny' side of life.

CHAPTER VII

MECHANICS

As we all know, a car-mechanic works on motor-cars. It is a work on many people's 'fondest brain-child', because a motor-car represents their innermost wishes. When this 'child' of shiny colour, chrome and a personal independence needs to see a 'doctor', efforts are usually made at least on two sides in order to bring it back to life.

One side would be the dollars of the owner and the other one belongs to a 'car-mechanic'. When both sides come together, the chance of a recovery for a 'beloved car' is well and truly again on track.

Cars on the other hand are not all the same. There are: private cars of different sizes and brands, transport vehicles and high performance 'machines from hell', called also 'racing cars'.

And so differ also the 'comedian-car-mechanics', the fondest 'brain-children's' doctors. They are: the motor-mechanics, diesel-mechanics and panel-beaters.

1.) MOTOR MECHANIC

Let's the **motor-mechanic** present himself first:

Again, who works for a living, has usually an early day. Ryan, our motor-mechanic is here no exemption. The alarm-clock helps also him to start his work-day in time. The newly wed-couple lives in a rented flat, not far from Ryan's work place. His wife Silvia gets out of bed, too. She works in a shopping-centre to help save money for their dream-home.

Children are planned for later on, when their rental-situation has changed. They look forward to investing all their work into a home of their own, which can give them much more personal freedom in an increasingly closer world.

A toast with ham and a boiled egg is 'washed down' more or less quickly with a cup of hot coffee. Silvia, his wife, joins him at the breakfast table still dressed in her nighties. She usually leaves later when her shop-assistant-term comes up. Ryan likes to start his day in clean overalls. The one from the day before has been put into the washing machine. He comes home some days with stained work-clothes, but on other days, hardly any dirty marks are visible. It is Silvia who keeps the work-clothes in top shape, ironing them as well.

A medium sized car waits in the garage under the house to take Ryan to work, less than five kilometres away. Into the car goes the lunch box and a shiny, big thermos flask of tea, too, which Silvia prepared while Ryan was in the bathroom. The driver is a proud car-mechanic, who keeps the car in a spotless condition, as well mechanically as by its looks. During his apprenticeship, ten years earlier, Ryan was already told: 'If your car is not running well, you are not a good mechanic'.

Around seven o'clock in the morning, traffic is already heavy in town. Ryan takes a couple of shortcuts on side-roads in order to avoid delays from the traffic on main roads. On arrival at work, he joins other colleagues on a bench in the open next to a patch of green grass and a flower bed for a smoke: "How is your Missus treating you? Did she let you off the hook for another work-day?"

"You must be talking about your own experience! Aren't you?"

"I have no Missus who on pay-days waits behind the door with the broom-stick to 'clean the money out of me'."

"Wait until you come across the right woman and she will twist your head and heart, so that you don't know yourself any more. We all go through this. In the end, we even like it."

"The first bell of the work-shop is ringing, we better start our day without a 'headache'."

"You are lucky, still young enough to learn more about life. Let's get real, work waits for us." The big roller-door to the work-shop is open right up.

No cloud in the sky promises any rain to arrive soon. A light breeze finds its way through the building, taking some of the typical motor-mechanic-smell out through the back-windows. Right and left to the wider centre-passage are motor cars in a row either on the ground or partly lifted up on platform-rails. Behind against the wall are work benches and every now and then a red tool-trolley with drawers waiting for its owner. Ryan and the other work-mates make up all together twelve staff-members. Five of them, including Ryan are fully qualified motor-mechanics. The other five staff-members are apprentices, of whom each learns and works closely with a mechanic. A 'master-mechanic' overlooks the whole operation. He has done additional business-organisation-training besides having many years of experience not only in this workshop, but proven records from other places, too. Ryan would like to follow in his master's footsteps.

Before this is however going to happen, Ryan has to do much more continued work. The day is just another one for him like for everybody else. The car he is working on, waits silently for him. Not long after the start-bell rings, noise gradually fills the workshop. Voices can be heard, compressed air hisses from lines, at least one motor is soon put into life.

Ryan started to work on a motor the day before. Nothing looks like a motor any more after everything has been taken apart and laid out on the work bench, trolley and in plastic containers on the floor. Repair and re-building of a dismantled engine starts from the bottom. The apprentice learns here to clean all the parts, put them in groups together as they come out of the engine compartment. Not one single piece can go missing, otherwise the engine could fail to run again.

Ryan is doing the dismantling alone, because experience tells that more than 'one cook will spoil the broth', which means in a mechanic's world, no one will know any more on the assembly, who did what and where eventually something belongs to. Until everything is dismantled and cleaned, the overall inevitably picks up dirt and oil from the engine even under best precaution. When the cleaning in a kerosene-bath is done, controlled compressed air and rags have finished the process, then a clean and smooth work-process lies ahead. Instead of carrying dirt along with the whole job, it is good to do the dirty part of a job first and thoroughly. The main job can then flow easier; 'once done right, nothing can haunt you any more'. It is also the best answer a car mechanic can give to his work. On the white wall of the work-shop is written in big, blue letters: 'Good Organisation is Half The Job'!

The 'master-mechanic', or 'boss' as he is called, makes his round. Ryan has almost disappeared on a body-trolley under the car, when the 'boss' talks also to him: "I can see, you are right in the job. Does Tom, the apprentice, know what he is doing?" – Ryan's muffled voice answers from underneath the car: "Tom is a good kid and learns quickly."

"What about the job? Can we finish it today?" Continues the boss while leaning on the front-bumper in order to reach better down to Ryan.

"I can tell you first when I've checked everything and know that we have replacement-parts in house", shouts Ryan from under the car.

"When you need help, just let me know. Tomorrow is pay-day again and a couple of jobs need to go out. If needed, can you stay back tonight for another hour or two?" – Suggests the 'boss'. - "I'm flat out at the moment, soon I'll let you know where I'm with the job." – "Don't wait too long, so we can see whether the job can be finished today or not. I've more work waiting for you," explains the 'boss' while he moves on in the workshop. – "Tom, listen, bend down a little, so you can hear what I've to say. Tonight we work another two hours extra to get the job 'out of our hair'. Tomorrow, you can leave earlier, if you wish. The pressure is now on us." – The bell rings for morning-tea.

"I'd like to finish first under the car and then we can have our break. I don't want to go under the car a second time. When you are ready, give me also a hand here under the car." – Morning-tea is over in fifteen minutes and the bell calls everybody back to work. Ryan and Tom keep still wor-king. Another twenty minutes and they too can fit in a break. They are not alone in the recreational room of the company. Two other mechanics have also postponed their morning-break. A radio plays music from a local channel. Ryan keeps an eye on the wall-clock for the fifteen-minutes-break. Again back at work, a list is established in cooperation with Tom: "You hand me a clean part, I in-spect and mark it when something has to be done, either re-work or replacement. You watch and learn from there. When we've gone through, you go with the replacement-list to the store while I take care of the parts which can be re-worked on the lathe or mill. This is a job you will learn in your apprenticeship further down. Are you ready? Let's go for it!"

Almost everything is sorted out nicely, except for two parts the store cannot supply. Ryan informs immediately the boss about these shortcomings.

A 'Courier' is called to organise the missing parts from the nearby city. The parts arrive still before midday, so that Ryan can leave the re-work of parts and go back to re-build the motor from the bottom. Tom hands one part at the time to Ryan, a spanner, a socket, an extension, a clamp, a seal, a bush, special lubricant, a clean rag, a torque-spanner, cylinder-ring-clamp, a bore-gauge and so forth as requested. Occasionally Ryan reminds Tom: "Don't fall asleep, we want to be out of this place still today!"

Lunchtime arrives half past twelve. Everybody has now half an hour break. An electric oven can be used to heat up a lunch brought from home. One of the apprentices starts it a few minutes before others join in the lunch- or recreational room. When the weather is fine and not too hot, some of the staff prefer to rest outside in the little company-garden on a bench. Ryan doesn't join the others, he wants a real good undisturbed rest in order to regain enough energy for the day's longer hours. He places in the lunchroom therefore in front of him another seat, on which he can put his legs up and have a nap. This time around it is not the bell reminding Robert of the day's work that lies ahead. He is preoccupied with finishing the day's job. It's therefore no wonder when

Ryan is back on the job, his apprentice Tom has not shown yet up.

A hand-sign proceeds Ryan's call for Tom: "Come on, don't tell me you are tired, our day has reached only half-time." - Not only Tom is immediately on hand, but also the 'boss' makes his way towards Ryan.

"How is the job going? To me it looks quite good. If you need additional help, don't hold back, we are all here to help."

"Thanks, it's getting there, I should be all right." - The job continues as planned also after the lunch-break. Slowly but surely most parts have come together when the bell announces the end of a standard hour working day, at four o'clock in the afternoon. "We are going to make it! In an hour or so we should be ready to test the new motor. It will tell us what we've done is right or wrong. Let's have for five minutes a quick cup of tea, so that we can also tackle the last 'hurdle'. You've been so far a good help today. I can't wait to listen to the motor when it revs back into life."

"Are we on target? I'll stay back with you both in case you need something. Only John joins us tonight. His job has to be out first thing in the morning, too. You know how the banks are. They are the ones who make our money so tight." – "You know 'boss, I'm not good with words, but what I can tell you, the job is well and truly on target."

And indeed, a little after five pm. the moment arrived. With the turn of the key, the engine roared instantly back into life, continuously running smoothly after some minor adjustments with the help of a 'diagnostic-centre'. Electronics has taken today a foothold in cars, which gives car-mechanics problems keeping up with this constantly changing technology.

The car-mechanic who doesn't keep up with new techno-logies, finds himself out of work sooner or later. Repai-ring cars is no more a 'bolt and nut'- business. Electronics and computers have also entered the car industry. The good motor-mechanic should be able to work on car-models of the past as well as current ones. As not all motor-mechanics can master such a demand, it is only natural also in their profession that different levels of professional competency exist. It is also here where the 'comedian-situation' sneaks in.

'What a day! Especially for the apprentice to experience firsthand a bigger job to succeed. And on top of it, within a set time', thinks Ryan.

"A familiar sound tells me, the job is well done. When you are ready, come and see me in the office and I throw in a round of beer. Is Tom, our apprentice, 'big enough for a beer'? I'm sure he is! Who works well and hard, should have also a beer as a reward! See you all in my office."

"We put quickly the tools back where they belong to. Don't worry about the stains on your clothes. We wash our hands and that will do.

Tomorrow we better come to work again with a clean overalls. Let's go over to the office. The 'boss' is not often so generous," reminds Ryan the apprentice. John, the other mechanic is already with the boss when the two enter the office: "Is there still beer left for us? Or have you 'worked hard' on it already?"

"Come in, close the door, sit down and here is a beer for each of you. We don't drink more than that, because we all have still to drive home. Cheers! I want to show that I appreciate your efforts. We've plenty work, because we always do a good job for our customers, that's why they come back to us.

Every day a beer, is however not on, you know that. It would spoil the special occasion. Tom, our younger generation needs to realise in time where is a good effort, there is always a reward not far away.

Efforts have to be however consistent like you've proven again today. Thank you and make sure you make it safely back home. See you again tomorrow. Tom, you can start two hours later like Robert told you."

When arriving at home, Robert finds his wife upset: "Couldn't you give me a call that you come later home today? Dinner doesn't look too good any more after I tried to keep it warm for you several times.

Your job is nice and good, but what about my job at home?"

"Silvia, my darling, I'm so sorry! I've been flat out all day, thinking only how to get my job done without too much extra time at work. The boss threw also a beer in at the end of the day to show his appreciation how good the work went. Next time I try harder not to forget to give you a call when I'm going to be at home later. Can you forgive me, please?"

"Well this time around, of course I can, because you are my darling husband. Get rid of your work-clothes and when you come from the bathroom clean, I want a kiss from you." – "You don't have to wait long for the kiss, I'll be there in a moment."

"In the meantime, I'll see what I can do with our dinner."

At the table, dinner takes place as usual. Forgotten is all day's trouble. As it's later in the day, there is not much else the young couple can do but watch a movie on TV. Hobbies, like Ryan's soccer-playing and Silvia's tennis, are more for the weekend. Both share their leisure time.

When Ryan plays soccer, Sylvia watches, and on tennis, Ryan usually acts as an umpire.

At home in the garage is also a second car besides their own car. This second car is a repair and detailing job of Ryan, on which he works mainly when the weather is not good enough for outdoor activities.

This car is a piggy-bank for the family home. Every little bit will help, especially a newly-wed-couple. - A day is for Ryan over rarely later than ten at night. The next day arrives for sure and if a motor-mechanic wants to keep his job, he has to excel at his daily work. There is not much room for errors in a tight 'dollar-chase'. One who can perform day by day, is in, the one not performing consistently, is simply out of a motor-mechanic job. Also here money drives a worker's existence.

To play by the rules of the trade, is the 'comedian-demand'. Failure to follow the rules is a direct responsibility of the individual motor-mechanic. There is no one else who could be blamed. What it really means, is a tough experience in the 'real world'. Not all people have this direct connection between work and responsibility. A motor-mechanic won't walk away from his job-responsibility with a 'golden handshake'.

2.) DIESEL-MECHANIC

How does a 'Diesel-Mechanic' compare with a 'Motor-Mechanic'? With an open mind, we can also watch and listen to other people's daily lives, have then a good chance of either picking individually some facts or understand the facts brought to our attention.

I, the author, can certainly not claim to be the only one who has heard this difference between a Motor- and Diesel-Mechanic: 'The size of spanners make the difference'. So what does it tell? A Diesel-Mechanic-spanner is usually bigger, because diesel-engines drive mostly big 'movers' like trucks, trains, tanks and ships. Most of these 'movers' won't fit into a motor-mechanic-shop. Trucks alone can have engine sizes of passenger cars, not to mention diesel engines of ships, which can rise with all its components almost to the size of a house.

When talking sizes, it can be assumed that 'Diesel-Mechanics' need strength and stamina for their 'bigger spanners'. There are however fundamental differences between a petrol- and diesel-engine. This difference has also sparked a specialisation in the two professions, motor-mechanic and diesel-mechanic. We can now see to what extend a diesel-mechanic differs from his fellow-motor-mechanic: The beginning of a work-day would only differ from person to person.

Mainly at work, differences will show up more or less. In this 'comedy' Ron is our diesel-mechanic to have a closer examination. The workshop, basically a big shed of corrugated iron construction, is located on the outskirts of the town. Roller-doors on one side go up high enough allowing also big trucks to enter the workshop. Except for one booth, the other four booths are occupied with a truck of a different brand and different dimensions.

Ron received the night before a traction engine of a Mack-truck in his booth involved in a road-accident. The tires were also therefore damaged. The tyres are undone, but not removed before the truck-body is lifted onto the hydraulic platform for a closer inspection. Ron calls his apprentice: "David, I want you here, right now! You prepare the impact socket for the wheel-nuts to undo only slightly. We do not want them off at this stage. I'll be back in a minute." – David is keen giving the impact-socket a first go on the nuts of one wheel. Ron returns, telling the apprentice: "You still have to eat a lot more and grow before you can operate this equipment. Let me have a go and I show you how it's done."

Not even Ron can loosen one of the nuts. - "The 'bastards' have rusted-in and haven't been undone for ages. We try now another way. If this doesn't work, we have got a problem. Get the ring-spanner for the nut and I'll bring our last hope, the three meter high-tensile channel bar. I secure the ring-spanner first on the nut while you push as hard as you can the end of the extension bar. You shouldn't waste our time pushing it into the wrong direction. Anti-clock-wise is the right direction. – Is that what you call pushing hard? I get somebody to secure with you the wheel-nut. I give it now a go. – 'Holy cramoly'! These 'bastards' don't want to come loose! Spray more WD-40 lubricant on all nuts. Use for a couple of times again the impact-socket." – Ron says to a fellow-worker behind him: "Give us a hand please. Two of us should be able to crack the 'bastards'. – Heave-ho, once more, heave-ho! Here it comes! One is undone! - Let's do the rest the same way. One good thing is, we've managed so far and don't have to resort to 'butcher's –work'. You know what I mean with that?"

Ron asks his 'mate'. "When everything else fails, the chisel and the big hammer are the last option on a tight rusted nut. Then the nut cannot be used anymore and has to be replaced." - It takes four people almost two hours to undo on three wheels eight M40 hex-nuts. The same job on a passenger-car takes for one person normally a few minutes only. Here is already the first difference between work on a passenger car and a 'big-mover'. – The day starts already with a 'sweat-job'. As it is sum- mertime, a short break with a cold drink out of a thermos-flask from home helps to restore some lost energy. David, the apprentice even goes under the cold water-tap wet- ting his hands, arms and face in order to cool down. The temperature climbs up in the work-shop by the hour despite its high ceilings. Ron plays down the heat, telling David: "You get used to it, don't worry! We've seen worse! 'Mate', you work in the Australian Outback, then you know what heat is, this is nothing!" – Off goes the job on the truck again. This time around in the engine compartment. Access to the engine is only given when the truck-cabin is swung from a gantry to the front. Everything is big here, which requires cautious attention by everybody in order to prevent personal injuries. It also matters, how something is done and in what sequence. Something done the wrong way round, means, double the work.

A platform with safety railings is brought into the place from right behind next to the motor. Ron reminds the apprentice David: "You make sure, no tool is dropped. We all have only one 'good head'!"

Morning-tea and lunch-time arrive so quickly that it almost appears as if only little was done on the truck. Most of the morning hours went into finding out what caused the diesel-engine to stop during the road accident.

Finally, Ron breathes a sign of relief: "I got it, this will be a big job! – I let the 'boss' know, so he can go back to the customer with an estimate. - In the meantime, you do the necessary cleaning on the engine. - Wait a moment, the boss is on his way. – "So how is our 'patient'? What are the findings? Did somebody else had a look, confirming your in- spection? If not, I join you in order to save time." – Ron mentions his findings from his list point by point while also the 'boss' climbs on to the platform confirming each step. The 'boss' has many years of practical experience in diesel-mechanics, he doesn't mind to come to the party and make his 'boss-hands' dirty. He likes to say:

"We are here to do a job. Dirty hands are nothing to worry about. We wash them and can give a 'King' again our hand. – Your inspection-list is ok., I take it into my office, do the figures and let the customer know what the job will cost him. I should be back with the go-ahead in the next half an hour, I'll let you know. You can have your lunch-break a bit earlier, right now." – While the rest of the workshop joins in the lunch-room, the 'boss' comes to see Ron about his truck-job: "Thumbs up, the customer has agreed on our quotation. The only thing we need to tell the customer is, when the job is done. You come and see me after lunch and tell me your estimate." – Ron cuts his lunch short by a few minutes. He is a bit nervous about the timing of the job, thinking by himself: "What can I tell the 'boss' without putting too much pressure on me? If it's too much time, he knocks me back. Too little time on the other hand gives me the 'shits'. I rather go somewhere in between and see what the boss says." – Ron heads then for the office to see the 'boss': "Are you ready to listen what I've to say?" – "Go ahead, I'm ready to listen!" Responds the 'boss'. – "How about four weeks? I think the job needs this time." – "Good thinking! The customer however has a different idea. I stand by my people and we organise something to get the job out in three weeks. You are the team-leader. Another trade-person off the shop-floor will be under your supervision during those three weeks. What do you think? Can we do it?'

"I can give it shot and try my best." – "I like to hear this! What I also do, I put a bonus aside for special required efforts. We've prepared the job and don't want the job to go now somewhere else with our information. The world has been crazy in the past and doesn't want to get any better! What I however know, we can win the 'battle' with our people. I leave it with you. Any help needed, do not hesitate to come and see me. I'll send Collin over to you. He'll be your right hand. You should be okay to work with him together." – Ron leaves the office in a thoughtful mood: "We'll see if it's true, 'we shall not count our chickens before they are hatched '. Now it is time for action, we can think about it afterwards." - Ron has a gulp out of his thermos flask in the lunch-room before returning to the job. Here he finds Collin and the apprentice ready waiting for him. – "Well, I can see, you are already 'on the ball'. I quickly discuss the job with Collin so that we don't 'stand on each other's feet'. Remember, organisation can be half the job! Heavy work like the one we have now in front of us, requires good thinking before we do something the wrong way round. We cannot afford to do things first half and then right. Let's not forget to communicate with each other in order to avoid misunderstandings. This is by the way not the first time, we tackle together a tight scheduled job. - I've said enough for now, if somebody else wants to say something, do it rather now, before we put our sleeves up." – "How about overtime and work on the weekend? I only hope, we won't go over the top. Can we arrange the overtime in daily turns?" asks Collin with the apprentice's support ".

"You know, much can be done, let's stop talking. Where there is a will, there is always a way," replies Ron.

All kind of tool-sizes are now used, including the lifting gear of a gantry which runs on top of the workshop from one end to the other. Not much is spoken any more. Even the apprentice learns best from watching and giving the crucial additional helping hand just when needed. The diesel-engine job requires the same attention to organise work-operations in order to proceed effectively and safely like a petrol-engine job does. For such a reason, the job-start is crucial in order to advance quickly, so that the real extend of the work becomes more visible. Parts have to be sent out for re-conditioning, or new parts have eventually to be organised as well locally as from overseas. Parts can neither go missing nor end up as left-overs if the job goes to plan.

Ron is also an excellent leader. When a job is urgent, he keeps working rather slowly but steady in the eyes of an outsider. This way he prevents unnecessary time-consuming rush-errors. Ron demands the same from his work-'mates'. – At the end of a long workday, including two hours overtime, the truck-job looks like a battle-field'. Parts seem to be all over the place, however in an order which only the men, who are on the job, can control. The 'boss' had to leave earlier, telling Ron: "The next days, I'll be staying back with you, today I've got a family-commitment. You lock the place and I'll see you tomorrow."

At the end of the day, when the three have stopped also working, Ron looks with satisfaction at their 'building-site': "Well done boys, it's enough for today. Let's go home, too."

Tom, the apprentice has been very tired in the beginning of his apprenticeship after a day's work from standing long hours paying attention and especially handling heavy stuff. Now, a bit more than a year later, he has learnt to stand up to the diesel-mechanic challenges.

After work, he pursues still regularly his own interests. Nowadays, the older 'bloke' is the one who needs a good rest after work. Ryan feels on some days the 'pinch' of the heavy work as he gets older. When he comes home, Silvia, his wife knows at a single glance how Ryan's day was. She is all smiles and when Ryan smiles back, the day was a good one. Today Ryan smiled back. He doesn't feel ready yet to do something else during the few remaining hours of the day. "Let's have a quiet evening after dinner. I've cooked one of your favourite meals for tonight, lamb-roast with rice and broccoli. A beer is already on the table. What do you think?"

"You are so good to me, tell me, how your day was."

"You know, it was my day off, so that I could do the shopping, bring our home up to scratch and what else was it? Well, time flies too quickly. You just turn around and that's it. You know, when it is quiet, I like reading which I also did today. – To go out, we leave rather for the days you come home earlier and the weekends are also there to do what we like best. If you don't want to read tonight, just after dinner comes a movie about the African wildlife. So we can have a nice time together." – "I know now, why I love you so much! You are the best that has ever happened to me. After a day's hard work, your smile is all I need, how could I be happier! After dinner I'd like to share our happiness together, the movie can wait."

When you think the work-day passed quickly, the evening goes even quicker. Time for a night's rest is knocking at the door without failure. The next day will be also for Ryan another one, during which he has to stand up to the diesel-mechanic-challenges again and again.

3.) PANEL BEATER

A panel beater is in many cases a 'motor-mechanic' who does everything on a car: not only what the name 'panel beater' indicates, beating damaged panels back to their 'former glory', but at the same time to fix every-thing else. To cover this panel-beater-work, authorities have introduced different licences. This means, licences or not, it will do the job in many cases, depending on panel-beater-skills and a business-reputation. – Damaged cars find usually their way to a panel beater. A panel beater's day is neither more nor less demanding than that of car/diesel-mechanic.

I let here the panel beater Geoff to tell about a typical work day: "Not much different from other trades people, I start my work day at seven in the morning. I've got out of the bed already two hours earlier, starting the day walking in the company of my favourite dog. The other three dogs stay back with my wife Lisa on our property. Back from a neighbourhood-walk, some other things are done to get my day started: first the lorikeets, cockatoos and kookaburras are fed in a dedicated place between a group of Eucalypt trees. Then it's the chooks to have their grains. Lisa lets the dogs meanwhile out of the house. She prepares food for the dogs outside and breakfast comes then on the table for me and her. Lisa does the work in the house and around the property while I bring the money home from panel beating.

Half an hour drive to work with the car is no problem for me. I rather live in the country, far enough from the town and work. I keep the car in a good running condition myself, so that the link between country and town can easily be maintained. My wife Lisa has a small car of her own, making her more independent in a relatively remote country-side. We both think: 'only go to the town when we want, but not have the town with us'.

A change from work to a life on a rural property is a reward enough for me to drive daily the extra miles to work and back home.

It is already daylight most of the year, when I leave home. I usually arrive first at the panel-beating-repair-shop in the southern outskirts of the town. In case I don't make it in time, the foreman of the work-shop has also got the key to open the gate of the completely fenced property. The office- and workshop building is alarmed. Only I and the foreman have the code to stop the alarm.

At seven am. sharp, the roller door to the workshop is opened. Cars stored overnight in the building are partly moved outside in order to allow access to cars in a work-process. People who have damaged their cars mostly in road accidents have brought plenty work in. When it comes to money-terms or even business profit, this work-load should not mislead. The reality is that mainly one insurance company drives the intake of damaged cars into the workshop. I'm the boss here. Every day is a challenge, not only for me but for all my staff in order to satisfy insurance-company-demands and also customer expectations. I have many years of experience in the panel-beating-trade and worked up my way from a modest beginning as an apprentice to a workshop-manager, giving still a hand where it is needed.

Despite administrative work, I also overlook work on the floor. One of the first measures when a damaged car is delivered either by the company's own pick-up or a contractor, the car's damage is to be documented. This is today best done with technology of video-imaging.

An estimate of the repair-job is emailed to the insurance company for approval. Insurance companies have for a car also binding regulations of time-limits to be put back on the road. Customers without insurance-proof have to pay usually a deposit with a repair-order.

During every day finished cars move out and new repair work moves in. Twenty staff work in the company under the supervision of the foreman and me. The foreman reports to me regularly on work-progresses.

It is amazing for an outsider to see how a damaged car goes into the workshop and comes out like new. Lots of skills, tricks of the trade, including a know-how of each car model go into a repair-job. Some damaged car-parts can be restored to their former glory with a careful form-work. Parts with more extensive damage are replaced, because a restoration work would be too time-consuming. Even a car-frame can be restored to a certain degree to its original shape.

People on the floor are working in teams of three to four on a car. One experienced panel-beater is heading every team. Damaged parts are stripped from a car, listing of required new parts is done and put on order straight away. Another team works on the parts which can still be used for a restoration, involving: form-work, sometimes fine-welding, grinding, pre-polishing. The third team helps putting the putty on the panels, with finish-polishing and spray-painting in a special booth before the panels are baked in an oven.

People on the floor have different qualifications. There are three apprentices on varying levels, six staff members are fully qualified panel beaters of which two have a special welding licence. Two more of the staff have an auto-electrician licence, whereas two others have experience in mechanical work on cars. The rest is casual workers with the prospect to become permanent employees.

Automotive electric work has to be done by a staff-member who has a current licence. It's amazing how many electrical wires run in a car hidden behind the dash-board and panels. After accidents, the whole wiring of a car has sometimes to be replaced because of hidden short-circuits.

Work-pressure is very much on daily, because of the timing dictated either by insurance companies or by customers.

During restoration-work, customers often claim the use of a rental car, which every party wants to keep for a limited time only. In the end, when the customers picks up his car, the only expectation is, the car looks like new. Most of the time this can be achieved, but in a few cases, the customer forgets what his/her beloved car looked like when it was delivered to the panel beater shop. I accept the rule that 'the customer is always right'. Therefore I'm always friendly and try to understand the customer to the point explaining also the panel-beater-shop position: 'We can do work, but no miracles'. The panel beater is here the 'comedian' of the customer, too.

Every twentieth car leaving the shop on time and the money which was quoted has been met, a barbecue is thrown in fortnightly on Fridays after work. "Then my favourite words are: A work-horse should have its feeding trough from time to time filled with something good." All the rush and work-pressure from the day are left behind and everybody can then have his share of a successful fortnight.

Staff members can talk about other things than work and find out that they all work for nothing more or less than to make a living as good as possible.

Extra hours are almost a must, so that the jobs can move better out of the workshop in time. Money is also here the order of the day. A job going out, means, money goes into the bank to pay the bills and most importantly the weekly wages of the employees. Every week is a tight money-race. Any room is hardly left for mistakes or delays in scheduled panel beater's work. A day's end is a relief for every worker, who is in the 'panel-beating-game'. The 'comedian' takes here sides with the insurance companies, the banks and last but not least with the customer.

So when the day is over and I can lock the place, all is well again. I then drive after peak-hour-traffic and arrive mostly at home with a little daylight still hanging around. Not enough time is usually left during the week late in the afternoon to do some work at home, even if necessary.

Some days are wearier than others. The weather plays its role, too, which can largely determine the rest of a day. On this late afternoon, the weather is still too good to stay indoors. The heat during the day has for a change receded early enough. I can therefore quickly forget the pressure from work and stroll with my wife Lisa on our property accompanied by our four dogs. The dogs love to chase a branch, or rock we throw away from us as far as possible. This is exercise time for all of us. Everything else around us settles for a peaceful night. Next to the little dam, the Ibises flap their wings hastily to get away from the curious dogs. The moment Lisa and I turn with the dogs back to the house, they return to the banks of the dam circling and swinging in the air. There, two cheeky kookaburras wait for their daily meat-morsel near the house entrance on an acacia-tree branch.

In case I come out of the house late, they remind me with their funny laughter that it is kookaburra-feeding-time. The birds make also sure, nothing falls on to the ground where the dogs are already waiting.

The birds' skilful dive from the tree almost never misses a piece of meat which I throw towards them. When I've no meat left, the kookaburras know it and take off disappearing in the nearby bush for the night. Nature gives also for Lisa and me the best relaxation after a day's work.

We have only to remember it.

I continue my round on the property to the chook-pen, topping up grains and water before the sunset. The chooks have already settled on a perch in front of their house for the night, clucking quietly and happily with each other.

Next to the chook-pen is my corrugated iron-shed, which holds my home-workshop. I cannot help but pay it a quick visit also today. I turn the lights on and what can I see? My new model-aircraft on the workbench. I'm fascinated again in an instant. The small paint-tins wait for me on the workbench next to the model to apply the finishing touch.

I don't hesitate to continue where I left my model-aircraft before. The time must almost have been forgotten, when Lisa calls with her loud voice from the house: "Dinner is ready!" – 'It can still wait a few minutes longer until I've finished at least one colour ', are my thoughts.

Just when I'm ready to switch the lights again off in my work-shed, Lisa is next to me: "Can't you hear when I call you? What the hell is going on? I'm all day on my own, prepare a nice dinner when you come home, so that we can enjoy some time together! You don't seem to value my work much at all? Won't you?"

What can I say: "I'm so sorry! I lost a count of the time. You know how proud I am of my model-aircraft. It gives me so much joy after a hell of a day at work." – "How about me? Can your model-aircraft give you a nice home and dinner? Come on, let's go and forget about it!"

"I realise only now that I've missed even today's news. Well, whether I watch today's news or not wouldn't make a heck of a difference. The world will be still around tomorrow. Instead of the news, you can say now, what you like us to do tonight." – "How about, we leave also a movie aside tonight and have instead an early night. A good night's sleep wouldn't do any harm. The heat during the day makes everybody tired. Come on, we can read a little bit in bed until falling asleep. It's almost ten o'clock. I'll finish in the bathroom first and wait for you in our cosy bed."

Another day is over also for our panel-beater Geoff and his wife Lisa. Other days will follow not exactly on the same path, but still in a company of the panel-beater-'comedians': customers, banks, money, mishaps and unpredictability of men & materials.

MECHANICS-CONCLUSION

One more thumb up for a motor-mechanic who can keep the 'comedian' in check, hot on his heels. – Why not on her heels simply, because motor-mechanics are still a man's-domain. After reading also this chapter VII, the question here is not only about to like or not like.

Everybody should ask himself/herself also this question: How much do I really know about these 'daily-battlers'? Somebody who denies it to be a 'battle', should give it a go, no matter how close or far from this 'game', he/she will no doubt find quickly out, why it is called a 'battle'.

Nobody is really spared a 'life-battle'. The further such a 'battle' seems to be in the moment, it will catch up with us more certain later on. In the end, "fate renders us all equal".

'Real knowledge' about other people, and not the 'latest gossip', can help us to better understand, whether we stand, on a risky, shaky or firm ground.

The knowledge of the "School of Life" is also here the 'right indicator'.

I, the author do not claim that my writing is the be-all and end-all, but a fresh picture for a fairer thinking about other people's lives. Let's get anew out of our 'glass-houses', take the 'blinkers' off and experience together the world around us as it is.

CHAPTER VIII

'POLITICIAN'

Which politician does recognise that also he/she is an 'comedian'? Most likely, none! Why? Because it would be out of step with the rules of 'political games': politicians are here to' bite the bullet' they receive from the public. This can only be done by somebody who has convinced him-/herself to be tough. The politicians see themselves surprisingly unanimously around the world: "we are 'hard workers' carrying much of the burdens and responsibilities of a society and therefore deserve due respect with a decent pay in return ".

Looking around the world, the fact is, we can hardly find a poor-politician. The 'red-carpet' is a standard in political circles, rolled out to return compliments, because already nature tells that "birds of a feather flock together".

1.) 'HONEST-BROKER'

Now let's give also a politician the chance to speak one day only.

John considers himself a successful politician. Let's see what he has to say: "I'm your member of 'Jarrah', a growing, prosperous suburb in our great State of 'Green-Meadows'. Thanks to my party's vision, we can all enjoy a better life today. I'm committed to my constituency and will continue to do so. It has never been easy going.

People come always first, they know me for almost three decades as a strong member of the country's leading party. At my mature age of the sixties, I've already learnt my lessons, which our community will only benefit from. I'm also a family-man, no 'hanky-panky' as every-body knows. To support my people is for me equally important as supporting my family. How could I other-wise know the needs of our community of which the family has been and will remain the cornerstone.

I give you an 'honest insight' into my daily life, which is not much different from anybody else's life except a continued struggle to keep the 'comedians' in their place. A politician is more exposed to public scrutiny than most people. It's like to cope with the punches received in a boxing ring. On one side are the public expectations, on the other side the politician, who stands up with his promises trying to keep a delicate balance of the 'possible' and 'impossible'.

Besides all this, a politician like me needs also a good night's sleep. When a caucus-meeting in Parliament doesn't rob my most night-hours, the day doesn't start much different from anybody else's. My wife Jodie is usually the first one to get up in the morning. Our two daughters need to be ready for school by eight o'clock in the morning. Jodie takes also care of transporting the girls with her car to the school. Before having breakfast with Jodie, I've to pay attention to emails, faxes and phone calls. During the night the answering-machine stays on, collecting calls which are put through first after breakfast. A coffee, toast and cigarette will get me started in the morning. Jodie has a more healthy breakfast taking her time while all these messages, enquiries and calls can't wait for me to pay my attention.

First thing is to visit on my laptop my daily organiser. What does it tell me today: Ten o'clock am. a community meeting for the homeless in the Lake-Park / eleven o' clock, the council presents a petition for a new housing-development / in the afternoon, the local hospital requests an extension for its surgical department, more beds, more staff / later in the afternoon, the party meets to discuss the strategy of the upcoming election / on a previous day a request from the public High-School could not be attended and is again on today's program. I've to find out, when I can fit it in.

As this was not enough, emails, faxes and phone-mes-sages are waiting for my attention, too. Tomorrow, I've to go to the Capital for a compulsory caucus-meeting. I tell myself: tomorrow is another day, today is the one to tackle. Some days I feel like I've been asked too much. I've then no other choice but to set priorities for my day's program. What cannot be done today, comes on a 'back-burner' and has to wait for another time. I remem-ber in the early days of my political career that I didn't know sometimes where to start and stop any more with a packed day's program. Experience has meanwhile told also me that 'no soup is eaten as hot as it is cooked'.

Somehow even things we don't like, can give us a helping hand, if we don't let pressure get the better of us. To forget something, is a strong human nature. Therefore it's not only me who gets caught from time to time red-handed, but other people, too.

We only need to get to know each other a little better which can help everybody a lot. Over the years, I've learnt to listen to other people and haven't made the mistake to go it alone. It is here where mistakes become obvious, eventually haunting and punishing the 'origina- tor'. Some learn from their mistakes, some don't. For my part, I still try to learn even at my age. - I better get back to my day's program and see, what can be done. First, there was the homeless-issue, which I consider an awkward one, because it shouldn't be here in the first place. But it's here and we've to face it. I rather address sensitive issues like homelessness with a low profile without evoking feelings that authorities are out of touch with other people's problem. Instead of an official formal suit and a tie, I get dressed for this occasion more casual. I listen again first what other speakers have to say, so that I know better where I stand with my official concept. No matter what words are chosen, nothing leads past the realities: No one will give away his home for others, or homeless people cannot expect to have their case heard without some kind of contribution; for instance, to help building homes also for them. Nobody else in the society gets a 'freebie', why should they have one. I'm caught here in the middle of the debate, safeguarding the 'money-tap' of the government and at the same time trying to keep up the hopes of an affordable, practical solution for the homelessness. Words had to be carefully selected on all sides not to unleash controversy. Nevertheless, in the end, I'd to leave for the next appointment with the Council. Here I better change into a suit and tie.

To do so, I quickly sneak into the Council's rest-room to get changed. It appears to me that all negotiations with different parties boil down to a simple formula: first listen and then talk. Between the hospital-appointment and party-meeting, I managed to fit also in the long overdue visit to the High-School Principal just before school finished. All in all, my day went again quickly.

Lot has been said, it remains to be seen, what actions can and will follow. I'm not ashamed to acknowledge feeling the constant attention towards community issues which make me tired rather sooner than later.

My mobile phone didn't stop ringing either during the whole day. Messages on its message-bank are waiting to be addressed at home if not answered already.

While I'm in town on foot, people do not only bid me 'good day', but come forward with urgent questions, too.

To show tiredness, is then inappropriate. People do not forgive for weak points especially of the others. I try to maintain always a positive approach with people, because it is quite well known that 'you are treated as you treat others'. This is also one important rule for a politician.

Somewhere down the line I can manage to get home almost every day not too late in the afternoon. Calls are then again collected on the message- bank. My mobile phone tells me who is calling, so that I can decide whether a call is important or can wait.

Jodie is in our home our quasi-'Interior Minister', whereas I'm our 'Exterior Minister'. It means that I do the work outside and Jodie mainly at home. This way we have time for our family when I come home. I must admit, this is the old-fashioned way how a family lives, nevertheless a practical approach. I also believe, we can't have it all what we eventually dream of. Otherwise we put too much unnecessary pressure on us and our families. To be contented is a value not to be underestimated. My constituency is free to hear about my principles, because a politician stands in people's eyes for what he/she believes.

It's the old story to show an example, if you want to be heard and have followers. Our children listen and follow us only when our example can convince them.

Home-coming is for me always rewarding. The wife and the children give me a hearty welcome.

Politics can then wait for another day. Family is now the focus for the rest of the day. Twice during the week, the children visit the indoor swimming pool, where they also meet some of their friends from school. The other outing for them is the Girl-Guides.

We like to play tennis together on the weekend. And when the weather is not good enough for outdoor-activities, reading, listening to music, watching movies is on. It is also a good opportunity to put everything in order, especially the children's rooms. Outside the house the lawn is often waiting to be mown and the weeds in the veggie-garden need to be pulled out, so that weeds don't overgrow the vegetables.

School is the children's entry into a professional life later on. Not only Jodie checks and helps on the children's progress, but also I do. We both encourage our children to pay also a visit to the local library in order to broaden their knowledge from an early stage. A family home cannot accommodate as many books as a library can. It shouldn't prevent us from becoming a 'book-worm', what a library is for.

The more we know, the better we understand. Also a politician needs to understand people in order to win them over for a common task. It boils mainly down here when it comes to dealing with people, it doesn't matter which age or social stand.

I can't say much else about my day as a politician who lives in and with a community, except that also my day should end with a good night's sleep. Jodie and I do not encourage our children to spend late nights outside our home, because too many uncertainties are waiting for teenagers at night to catch up with them. We see too much these things happening around us. I hear from parents constantly that they lost contact with their children. All this has become a great community-concern and we all can't just sit on the fence watching our children caught between their families and an unforgiving outside-world. I'm ending here my talk."

The focus on community-needs should be the concern of a 'popular' politician, who negotiates with all parties without overcommitting people's representation or people themselves.

The politician who has spoken here, is probably the 'honest-broker' in the political 'game' as many people would like to see every politician.

G.B. Shaw had already said: "I'm afraid we must make the world honest before we can honestly say to our children that honesty is the best policy." Unfortunately 'words' won't represent 'honesty'.

'Actions speak louder than words' rather points into a direction of 'honesty'.

2.) POWER-BROKER

Politicians differ from individual to individual as other professions do. What is a 'power-broker' compared with an "honest broker' in the political arena? Obviously 'power' is speaking differently than 'honesty' does. All the 'tricks' of a 'political trade' rather concentrate in 'power' and its expressions. Who is now the 'better politician'?

Let's find out and give the 'power-broker' a voice to her local constituency: "I honestly don't know, why we have this problem. It shouldn't be here in the first place. People of our great nation deserve something better than the current government has delivered so far.

Trust me and my party, the 'People-Party'. Your voice in the coming election will help us all. I promise to turn around what has been neglected for too long. The Nation battles price-increases without an end in sight. Under my Government GST will not be increased, families with children will receive an urgent needed tax-relief. The nation's hard workers will not be left hundreds of dollars out of pocket because of unjust increases in power-bills and rates - equal opportunities for all our children at school - pre-school subsidies for working parents - more training-places in the industry - more money for the universities and easier access to higher education for all – a restruckture of the health-system - more doctors, nurses and hospital beds. Our roads aren't getting better either. A long-term plan needs to be developed for better roads. – I could go like this for ever, which only shows in what a poor state our economy is left. The economy is the driving power, paying for all these community-requirements. We change the 'dole' from a social benefit into a 'work-'dole'. Incentives have to be created to make again work attractive. The Nation's deficit has to come to a halt. There is no future if the government and we all keep spending money endlessly.

This is only the beginning of what I've to say to this honourable House Of Representatives. I pass the word now on to the government-party."

A response from the other side is almost predictable: "Who is going to pay for all that? Money doesn't grow yet on trees just to be picked. If you want money these days, you've to take it away from somewhere else, where a shortfall will only appear sooner or later. Since when are people so badly off according to the opposition. The country is still around and people go about their lives as they have ever done. Let me tell you now what we've done when you were only all mouth in government …."

An opposite picture is drawn and a 'tug of war' can begin. Such is life in politics. The political 'power-broker' is the one who brings the 'bitter pills' into the 'political game': people like the 'sweet taste' delivered by the 'honest-broker'. 'Look at people's mouth and find out what they want to hear', is the 'honest-broker's' rule. As long as people hear what they like, they keep quiet. The better the 'bitter pill' remains hidden from public scrutiny, the better are the chances of winning government. A 'power-broker' is the politician who listens to the power-groups of a society. It is a well-known fact that, where money is, there is power. Therefore money has the power. And where is no money, there is no influence. After a lengthy 'tug of war' in Parliament and outside, the 'pendulum of public opinion' swings surprisingly consistent to the 'power-broker's' side. Why this is so, because money can buy almost anything, even votes, depending on how entrenched in a society 'corruption' is; the 'Holy Trinity of Politics 'has always been: "I know something about you, I need something from you, I have something for you".

POLITICIAN-CONCLUSION

Now that both politicians, the 'honest-' and 'power-broker' had their say, it needs also to be said: Outside their private lives, the two politicians can adopt very different views and strategies, whereas their lives run privately 'more on an even keel'. The private daily life of the 'power-broker' doesn't differ much from that of the "honest-broker'.

Here both politicians have family and cherish their private lives very much. They are also past their fifties, they can look therefore back on some life-experiences which are always good, but not everything. Experiences can easily mislead, because knowledge is here in opposition to ignorance. The younger politician is naturally more risk-taking, which requires eventually the cautious circumspection of the more experienced politician. A bit more young enthusiasm wouldn't do any harm to the older, experienced politician, visa-versa. One is on the 'gas', the other one on the' brakes' keeping politics on a road without too many obstacles. Life in politics is said not to be easy, because controversies out of public life are not going away, they knock with insistence at the doors of politicians. Here are the 'comedians' of politicians from which they can't escape, keeping them at bay is rather the answer.

CHAPTER IX

"GARBO"

"Garbo", what is it? How many people will ask this question? Here is the answer: "Garbage –Collector" is probably more commonly known.

Much in life is also here a question, whether we like something or not, because there are necessities like "garbage-collectors".

'Garbage' is something we dispose easily. Its 'collector' is however in a public opinion sometimes 'caught in the middle of the pie'. Simply an opinion, is also here not good enough, that's why I better give our 'garbo' Gavin a voice to explain himself in a typical garbage-collector-day: "Emma, 'kill' the "bloody" alarm-clock for us, if I can't have a bit more of a rest, this day will be a 'pain in the a..' I've to look only out of the window and the rain gives me again the 'shits'." – "You stay where you are, I can't be in bed much longer once daylight comes through the windows. I'll start my day and 'knock you out of bed' quicker than you can count to two. Men are hopeless, what would the world be without women?" reminds Emma, his wife. – "Don't play the 'boss', leave me alone!" replies Gavin half-angrily. – Time to start the day comes and Emma storms into the bedroom: "Hi 'boss' …., ah, what can I see, he must have fallen out of bed already!" Emma is caught by surprise.

"No wonder I can't sleep when you are busy in the kitchen!" Gavin is shouting from the bathroom. – "You better hurry, your coffee is getting already cold!" comes back from the kitchen. - Gavin plays finally down the morning's late start at the kitchen table: "What do we want? Everything is fine! Just another day not only for me but you, too!"

Breakfast is cut short, so that Gavin can leave for work in time. Emma leaves sometimes later for her work in a supermarket after the flat is put in order at least a little bit.

The trucks in the company's depot have no understanding for late arrivals of their drivers. Garbage is an impatient 'customer' waiting on the road-sides to be collected on time. Any back-log in the garbage-collection would throw a daily plan out.

Gavin doesn't ride his motor-bike today to work, because it's pouring with rain. Emma gives him instead a lift with the only car the couple can afford. She returns home for a short time only before leaving for work, too.

Other truck-drivers have already arrived at the depot getting ready for a new day's garbage-collection: "Hi fellows, you must be early today!" welcomes Gavin his 'mates'. – One of the fellow-workers makes the point: "Didn't your 'old woman' let you off the hook in time? Your truck is waiting for you." – "Thanks, and I'll catch eventually up with you fellows sometimes on the road when our paths cross. Don't work too hard! "Is the message from Gavin who reports his arrival straight away in the office. – "Gavin is our 'sleepy head' today! Book yourself in for your shift and hurry, so that you can catch up with the others. Your district is the usual one, the Western Suburbs. Check your loading-gear on the truck, make sure you have enough diesel for the day, because the morning-drizzle will slow down everybody's operation anyway. You are a good worker. No doubt your day will go well. See you later, when you report back."

The operation manager sends Gavin with his truck on to the road.

Traffic throughout the town is already busy short after seven am. The area Gavin empties the waste-bins is well outside the main traffic. When he enters with his garbage-truck the first road, he can see right to the end, in front of each property two different coloured waste bins lined up on each road side. The hydraulic lifting-arms, which pick up one bin at the time are fitted on the left truck side straight behind the driver's cabin-door. Gavin also realises that not all bins are again placed properly on the road side. They are nowhere near in a line, giving Gavin a problem to operate the lifting mechanism on the side of his truck. Gavin says repeatedly to himself: "If people had to operate the lifting gear on my truck only once, they would never again place a bin incorrectly."

In fact, stopping the truck constantly in a driving direction and correct distance to the bin, is a good skill-training. To watch the forks coming down in the outside mirror towards the back of the bin as they go into a pocket lifting in a matter of two or three seconds the bin over the top of the truck's collection-container, requires good visual judgement from the driver. Despite a number of bins are out of a correct position, it very rarely happens that the forks miss a bin making it drop to the side. Gavin is alone in his truck. He cannot get out of the truck, put a bin with its contents back into a correct position and give it another go. His answer is: "Bins wrongly placed, won't be emptied. We have enough pressure to collect so many bins daily. It's all about money-saving. Don't get me wrong, I'm not talking about my money. There is not much more they can save. It's rather the public- money the Council likes to spend somewhere else. I wonder how much of it ends up in their pockets."

Where would Gavin otherwise end up when interrupted every so often during the stop- and go-collecting operation. People will quickly realise why their bins were not emptied. Sometimes it also happens unfortunately that people turn around and blame the driver for incorrectly handling their bins. It usually on the return-trip of the truck, when the other side of the road is served.

Often an angry house occupant confronts the truck driver: "Can't you do also my bin? What's wrong with you? I'm not paying my rates not to have my bins emptied by the Council!" - Gavin hates these people and rather bites his tongue instead of responding in a same agitated manner:

"You place your bin correctly next time and there will be no problem! I've a job to do!" – "You won't get away so easily like this, I'm going to file a complaint with the Council!" – "Do what you like, don't get me over the top. I'm only doing my job. You better think twice whether you want your bins to be emptied in the future. This time around I bend the rule if you bring your bin to my truck. Let's do it right next time. You will realise that it's no big deal. Imagine, everybody jumps up like you! Where would we end up?" - Finally this bin is also emptied, Gavin gets out of his truck cabin, gives the grumpy owner a hand on the ground and everybody's day is saved. Not only unpleasant meetings happen with local house-occupants,

There are fortunately also highlights during a garbage collector's day. Gavin remembers: "Last year in December, just between Christmas and New Year, a few people came to my truck handing me through the opened door-window a 'six-pack'. A handshake, well wishes and thanks for the service during the year followed. I couldn't ask for more recognition than that! What a difference people can make! There is no need to be grumpy! We are all here to do a job, which everybody after all should do.

The more we understand each other's job, the better we can help each other. Garbage collecting is neither the best nor the nicest job on earth.

What other choice have I got? I do my job to my best ability what gives me plenty confidence. Also my wife has a job and so we manage our daily life fairly well. Only my income couldn't get us far, but this is not me to blame, rather the constant increases of living costs. I know, we all are more or less in one and the same boat. Nobody is so much better off, whether a 'Garbo', Prime Minister or Doctor. I definitely don't want the other people's problems. I've got enough struggle on my hands to collect garbage.

On my daily collection run I meet many people, see in our community as much good as bad, so that I sometimes feel as if I were the most important person in town. There is hardly anybody who doesn't know me. And I know to appreciate it. Therefore I can look past some garbage –collection-problems, because people are for me more important than the rubbish I collect from them."

Back on the road to empty the garbage-bins: "First of all, there are two bins if not three, depending on the Council's organisation, mainly different in their colours. Usually a green one, is for dirt and general rubbish. The yellow one is for paper and recyclable items, whereas the third bin is often for glass. Each of the bins is separately picked by a different collecting-truck. I empty the green bins and later during the day another 'work-mate' picks the yellow ones with his truck. On the back of my truck is a clear sign: "Watch the constantly stopping and moving vehicle!" One eye has to look forward, the other eye backwards to the road watching traffic.

People overtake me occasionally like dare-devils in passenger cars. In my truck I know that I'm sitting higher from the road and my truck body is stronger than many smaller cars. I had a few near-misses but yet no real crashes, thanks God.

I wonder sometimes why "Garbos" cannot have a 'third eye' to watch besides the traffic in front and behind, also the bin pick-up with the lifting-gear. Well, perhaps to listen with the ears helps also a missing 'third eye'. If there were anything more to complain, it's the left-open bins because of too much garbage piled high up. I won't touch those bins. They are the ones ending up on the road with the rubbish all over the place.

Otherwise every bin is lifted over the top of my truck-container. The hydraulic system shakes heavily the upside-down bin only for a short moment in order to empty everything from the bin.

The bin is then placed into its previous position on the road, forks are returned and brought in action at the next bin on the road. All this is carefully controlled inside the truck's cabin with one hand on a 'lovestick' which moves into all directions as required. The operator has to have a steady hand to operate the truck's lifting gear precisely for the standard garbage bins. What really goes into the trucks container from garbage-bins is often a guess: heavy rumbling, liquids running into the container, bad smell are all indications that despite regulations people have dumped stuff which are not allowed to be disposed in garbage bins.

On hot days I can't wait to have the container full, so that I can drive to the 'dump' and get rid of the sometimes terrible smell from behind my cabin. Particularly when I stop, I better have the door-window up to keep anything unwanted out. Most truck cabins are these days air-conditioned keeping its driver at least cooler. If I can see something illegally dumped, I pull out my record book, make notes and leave one copy in the letter-box. People have then to go and explain to the Council what and why they have done something wrong. I haven't experienced it, but other work-mates have experienced that the truck container exploded from some mysterious dumped substance or caught fire. All this is hidden from the public, because a majority of people see only that everything runs trouble free in a garbage collection.

The truck container is emptied at least four times at the Council's 'dump', which is located in the East, outside housing estates." – When everything runs to plan, a 'Garbo's-day' is nearing its end when the garbage-collecting-area has been covered.

There are days, Gavin forgets to take a break, which he realises only later in the afternoon when suddenly tiredness overcomes him.

"No more driving", he then tells himself. "When really busy, one can forget time easily. Garbage doesn't go away, if not picked. Heavy rain for instance can upset a whole week's program. When falling too much behind the schedule, it is often decided to catch up with the garbage-collection earlier in following days and late nights. And if this doesn't fix the problem, work on weekends is likely to be scheduled, too. At least the money is then also better. It never happened so far in our town that garbage was left for days, nor for weeks rotten stinking in the streets. When this happens, latest then people get a better idea how important it is in communities to regularly dispose of the garbage."

Where are people, there is also garbage. "Garbos" are bound to do their daily duties and cannot leave before reporting back to the depot. Also much can go wrong with the truck.

To change to another truck is time-consuming, because the broken down truck has to be returned to the depot for repair. Thanks to mobile phone technology, the "Garbos" out in the field are constantly in contact with the depot, so that no one is left stranded. It's like a big family standing close together. Management is here very much responsible making the garbage-collection working, also here people are the main assets. Trucks and equipment can be repaired, not so easily failed people relations. "Garbos" can be strong together, but also become very angry people when managed wrongly. It's always the old management rule to listen to other people before making isolated decisions.

"I'm not on the 'management-side', I'm on the' receiving-side'. If they do their job right, I can work all right. That's how simple life can be.

Otherwise I don't mind saying that 'every dog has his day' and so do I feel today at the end of another day: I've made my day, the job is done and also my truck can rest in the depot. My wife Emma is already at home when I walk through the house door. The way she is waiting for me behind the door, I know straight away, her day was a good one. All it needs then is to give her a hug and we both know, our day was good. A man who collects garbage of other people needs at least one beer at night to get rid of all the dust and smell of the air surrounding a garbage truck.

On some nights I go out with Emma to see friends. Once a week I join the local basketball-team in the town's indoor sports complex while my wife Emma helps out in the RSL - club next door. So looks basically my day, the one of a "Garbo". How the day of my fellow-workers is, isn't really my concern. I suppose we all have to get up in the morning, struggle along each day and go again to bed. TV gives Emma and me after a day's work also some pastime. It's me who falls often asleep in front of the 'bloody' TV. But what can I do? Emma needs only to tickle me on the sole and I jump up straight away. The bedroom is just a few steps away, so that I can't miss the bed for a good night's sleep. Not much later, Emma joins me. Women are all the same, what men don't do, they will do. Emma wouldn't go to bed for instance before the kitchen is tidied up. I, on the other hand don't worry much about dirty dishes, because tomorrow will be another day and what was not done today, can easily wait until tomorrow.

It's a similar story with having kids: Emma wants them, whereas I'm not so keen. Those 'buggers' when growing up these days, they can easily become a pain in the butt. We only need to look into the neighbour's place what kind of trouble the kids can give their parents. We better pay our house-mortgage before committing ourselves to something else."

"GARBO"- CONCLUSION

How clear is this voice of a "Garbo"? Where is the 'comedian' hiding here? – Gavin doesn't muck around, he is rather a straight forward man:

"Garbage keeps your head clear", is his opinion. "Where would I end up, if I lost my head with the 'garbage' which other people keep in their heads; just think of our politicians.

Everybody would be much better off, if for instance 'political garbage' could be collected and dumped on a regular basis. Politicians keep their 'garbage' in. We the professional 'garbage-collectors' keep on the other hand 'garbage' out. Why politicians get away with all kind of their 'garbage', is a question I can't answer.

On another note: Our funeral-undertakers are probably our next of kin when it comes to job security. Not many people want our job. We are however indispensable, nobody has ever tried to do without us. 'Funeral-people' won't of course go about their 'collection' as straight forward as we the 'Garbos' do. They are much more sophisticated and earn therefore also more money. We 'Garbos' do simply our job as we are told and don't muck much around. "The 'comedian' is with the 'garbage'. The better the garbage is under control, the better the 'comedian' is kept at bay.

CHAPTER X

LAWYER / 'LAW-TWISTER'

In this collection of 'professional experts' the lawyer has also his say at the end of this volume one, at least. The end doesn't mean here something less impor-tant. There is actually no need to stress the importance of a lawyer's words. Has he/she therefore also the 'last laugh'? Let's find out where and how 'lawyers' spend their daily lives:

To be right, is granted exclusively to 'divinities'. A lawyer claiming his/her 'rightfulness', how close would he/she be to be 'divine'?

Are the 'comedians' still real in the lives of lawyers and 'law-twisters'?

1.) LAWYER

I let the 'lawyer' go first, the more commonly called legal person.

Whether lawyer or not, also Barry needs a good night's sleep, including his wife Amy. They are not in a hurry early in the morning like most other people, what they regard one of their privileges. The couple has no children yet. Professional careers have played in the last couple of years the most important role in the couple's life. Barry and Amy are both legal professionals. Barry has said ever since they met: "One and one makes two also in legal terms. We shouldn't have too many problems in our profession. We both should know what to expect from the legal side." – And indeed, this side of a coin has so far worked out well for them in their lives: the young couple, both in their early thirties, live in their own home, the mortgage is nothing to talk about any more, two flash new cars wait in the garage for them and holidays have become a regular pastime. – How about the other side of a coin in their lives?

The two legal professionals can afford a lengthy relaxing shower every morning. At the breakfast table, eight o'clock news are switched on, sparing the effort of an too early conversation. TV tells also them whether 'the world is still around'. When the news change to sports, it's time to leave for work, in the city-centre. The early traffic rush is still on. Barry and Amy work in different places but not far from each other.

It usually takes them three quarters, up to an hour to get there. They use one car, the other one remains locked away in the home-garage. Amy usually drives, so that she can drop Barry first off before parking in her company's specially reserved underground garage. Amy stops on the road side in front of a high rising glass-palace. She doesn't worry about the people-crowd pushing its way along the side-walk. She gives Barry a hug, demonstrating the affection lawyers can also have to each other.

Not even a kiss is missing. "See you tonight" is all what they say to each other. A desk amongst numerous others waits in an open office environment on a numbered floor for Barry and Amy likewise. Windows go around the entire office from the floor up to the ceiling. It's like in a showroom.

The only difference is that no one else is so high up in the area looking from another building into this office. On sunny days, plenty natural daylight reaches each office-place and yet there are fluorescent lights all day on from the ceiling. The only effect of these lights, no shade is created across the whole area. Does this tell, transparency is naturally given here? May be, a transparency within the office.

Amy tells a little about her work place: "Everybody who enters these premises can only do so if the bar-code-security at the entrance receives the right digits. It's here where transparency stops. Stacks of files are awaiting me on my desk. On each one stands in clear letters: Strictly Confidential! Here are legal cases prepared for court-hearings. Evidence is collected, put together and legally verified. It's all getting difficult once a case ends up in a solicitor's files. Outside in the community, people do quicker something wrong by law than it can be legally corrected again. My colleagues in this organisation are equally called 'lawyers' as well as 'solicitors'. 'Lawyer' is just the general term for a 'solicitor', a person who is qualified to advise people about the law and to represent them in court, and to write legal documents. As a 'solicitor', I'd be called probably by the public more a 'paper-tiger'.

Today, the age of computers, lot of paperwork is done on laptops and centrally stored in the organisation. Paper-work is still around as my desk can tell. When I sit in front of my desk, the pile of files on my left side is the one for me to go through, while the smaller pile on my right hand are matters in progress. Just looking at my desk, makes me go to the coffee-machine first, so that I can better think with some refreshments 'how to tame my paper-tiger'. Paper is known to be 'patient'.

When I however sit in front of my paper-pile, I feel sometimes that I am the 'comedian' who has to come up from underneath to get on top of a job. I must also admit, life as a solicitor is not meant to be easy either. Every-thing needs its time and therefore becomes expensive. To be 'right', is not cheap any more.

That's why I give my clients a personal advise: Think rather twice before you break the law again. But then, if all people thought that way, where should we, the solicitors be left?

Anyway, early in the afternoon, a case in court requires my attention. I give therefore my clients a call reminding them to appear in court in time. I hate nothing more than chasing a client, who didn't turn up at a court-hearing. Those people do not realise that they make matters only worse when they don't appear in court. This time around, my client appeared in court as it was expected."

Another hearing will only add 'food' to a 'paper-tiger'. More hearings will add to a bill, which grows always with time. A vernacular tells: when two are at logger-heads with each other, the third is the one who wins, and this is more likely the solicitors than anybody else. Law and money keep well together.

Who has neither law nor money on his/her side, is going to have at least a difficult 'battle' ahead. – "I stick to the rule outlined by the written law. My job is either to know or find the rules in order to determine what is before the law 'right' or 'wrong'. New 'interpretations' of a written law are a difficult territory. One must know by experience where this can lead to.

It's here where my husband Barry and I differ despite both having the same profession. Before I pass on the voice to my husband Barry, I'd like to continue talking a little more about my day at work. During the day we make suggestions on a board for meetings, which the head of our office then calls, allocating every so often a time to discuss not more than five minutes each legal issue brought up by colleagues. This is mainly to confirm the legality of issues. Our office has a standing reputation for good legal services. Team-work is the key. More than one opinion can only help reduce misjudgements, which in the 'legal game' can be very expensive and time-consuming. Speaking on my behalf, I rather have another opinion instead of going alone. Legal issues have become too complex to allow short-cuts in laying down verdicts. This is how my office operates, more on a safe side than with risks involved.

2.) 'LAW-TWISTER'

The office of my husband Barry operates differently. It is less specialised in legal terms preferably dealing with controversial issues.

I've discussed often with Barry at home about his side of the legal profession: "We've to have more of an open mind and shouldn't see solicitor-work narrow-minded. The 'legal-game' is driven specially by money. Why not take the 'pick of the bunch'? Nobody refuses a better pay. Solicitors are no exemption.

Just listen to the media or people-opinions on some legal matters as they happen to circulate publically. First a few 'media-slips': "Dad gives his teenage daughter a smack on the bum - Dad goes three years behind bar without parole. - A burglar is caught in action during a house robbery by the owner; the owner fights the burglar off, injuring the intruder, so that he ends up in hospital. The verdict is: 'The harm the owner inflicted on the alleged burglar is disproportionate. The owner is summoned to pay the medical expenses and damages. - The murderer was acquitted on not enough evidence and declared not to be responsible for his actions.

A 'lad' pinches the wallet from a lady's handbag. Another pedestrian watches it and intervenes. Instead of regaining the wallet, the pedestrian ends up with a blow into his face from the lad. Only intervention from other people stops the incident going out of control. Police takes the lad into custody. The verdict from a psychologist: 'the wallet was not sufficiently secured in the lady's handbag and the only twelve year old boy acted accordingly to his state of mental instability'. The lad was released on a good behaviour bond.

Here are also a few public comments on the legal 'game': "Don't believe what the 'law-twisters' say, they are only after your money!"

"There is only one winner, and that's them!" – "What is 'right' and 'wrong'? If you don't have the money to get the answer, better don't ask questions!" – "Solicitors are after your money and time."

"Time works in favour of solicitors, they can wait, the longer, the better their money grows." – "To see a legal person, costs you already an arm and a leg." – "Money is 'right', from the living or dead." – "One can rarely see a solicitor on a wrong side."

"How does all this add up?" Barry asks his wife Amy in one of their private conversations. He gives also a bit of an inside into a daily run at his law-firm: "All what I can say, law-firms are much the same.

Past their doors, everything is 'strictly confident'. I consider it like playing chess: every move has to fit a concept, and who hasn't got the better concept, is not in legal terms exactly 'check-mate', but will pay the bills. Our firm takes into account also the public opinion. If we don't win the other side over with better arguments, there is a saying to which we stick to: if the 'Pope' doesn't come to the 'church' any more, the 'church' comes to the 'Pope'. Our clients are our' bread' and 'butter'. No clients would mean no bread', no' butter' for us, the solicitors. Why not have 'Justice' 'blindfolded' in the eyes of our clients and take the 'veil' away only when needed. People, our clients, neither need nor want to come to terms with the 'legal rumbling'. They get only confused and lose trust in the legal system. To be honest, do all legal professionals really understand what they stand up for? The legal system has become so difficult that judicial power is split into too many directions. A return to a simple, true verdict has become time-consuming and expensive on top of it. How can we sell this to the public also in the future? Let the public also have more their say in legal matters! Independence of the legal system cannot lead into an isolation, which previously mentioned press- and public-examples, have originated from. My answer to legal 'stalemates' has become 'twisting the law' in order to let more light shine into it.

'Twisting' doesn't mean here to nip the system in the bud, not at all, but rather to make it more transparent, so that all sides have a better understanding, solicitors and clients as well.

A move out of the 'legal glasshouse' should not be prevented by signs: "Don't throw stones!" It can be then easier to recognise that other 'glasshouses' have opened their doors for 'team-work'. Without a team-work in the broadest sense, modern cars or aircraft couldn't be a reality.

The legal system has to do a lot of catching up in order to come in line with modern, necessary progresses. We still have one leg in the past and the other one tries to be in step with the present. A result out of this can only be instability. To avoid instability, the answer of my legal firm is 'twisting'. This is not a bad thing after all, let me give you therefore a better idea of my work-day. I still want to emphasize beforehand, this is not about undermining the work of my wife in the other legal firm. It shows rather that also legal-firms are to some degree different from each other. They are never the same.

I'm going to give a window into two cases, which I consider different:

3.) 'THE OLD SCHOOL'

The client has taken a seat on one side of a desk in one of the legal-firm's 'questioning rooms'. Opposite the desk sits a solicitor with a pile of files in front of him. The solicitor opens the top-file and asks the client:

'Are you such and such person? - The client answers all the questions - Are you aware, you have broken the law and I've to declare you guilty?' - 'Don't you want to listen to my side of the story?' Asks the client. - 'I've no time to waste, I rather tell you what is going to happen now with you. Guilty, no question, not produced evidence of your innocence. Did it happen or not? - The solicitor tries to find out.

'Well what should I say. Since I'm here, something must have happened, otherwise I hadn't been called in front of you. / Don't be smart. First of all, you better learn respect and call me respectful 'Sir'. This is the rule of law!' – 'I give a shit what you want to call yourself! '- 'I don't have to listen to such an indecent insult. Forget what you've said and we bring your case to an end. Say, I'm sorry!' - 'I can say 'sorry' as much as you like. What difference would it make? I won't keep you much longer, your case is closed. Sign here and you can leave. Be ready for your first court-hearing, we let you know. Don't try to stay away, you'd make your case only worse. Any question, better ask now.' - 'I better get out of here. I don't understand much anyway.'

4.) 'THE NEW SCHOOL'

Here the client is received at the door and asked to take a seat at a desk next to the solicitor. No file is on the desk. The solicitor introduces himself: "I'm John and would like to represent you at your court hearing. Your name must be Darren. Thank you for coming to see me. Together we'll do our best. How are you today?"

"I'm a bit nervous, but fine otherwise." – "I'm going to tell you, why you are now here with me:

Before I talk to you, I ask you to tell me honestly all you know about the case filed against you. Remember, you are innocent as long as not proven guilty. So, what can you tell me?" – "I didn't do anything wrong. The other person pushed me to the limits. I couldn't take any more of that and landed my strong left fist on his face. This made him shut up. What happened after that, I can't understand."

"Before going any further, you don't mind if I ask you some details like the place where this happened, what day and time, who else witnessed the incident?"

"The bloke is known to 'kick up a stink' wherever he turns up. Somebody had to stop him. The police doesn't know anything, they just took us both away, it was not fair. The other bloke didn't even hesitate to turn the whole story upside down by telling lies that I started the quarrel. If I meet that 'bastard' again I'll teach him another lesson!" – "May I interrupt you here? I got now a better understanding from what you told me. Was it said honestly? "-

"I bet, you can, of course! I've been all my life honest. You can ask anybody in town who knows me." – "I believe you, you are honest to me, that's why I'd like also to be honest to you: I can understand that you became upset, but I've also to make you aware that the law doesn't allow anybody, including me, your solicitor, to take the law into his own hands. If you had just reported the personal insult of a fellow citizen to the police, we had not to break our brains now how to get you out of this situation. I can do something for you but only if you cooperate:

You neither say nor do anything with regard to this incident. Avoid the other side and don't get involved in another brawl. They could try to prove their case, if you re-offend.

To say it clear to you, put yourself under no circumstances into a same or similar position. Just keep out. You are a strong man and can keep your word. Any complaints from the other side will make matters only worse. Have you got more questions? Do you understand everything I explained to you?" – "I reckon, you are a nice bloke, I'm easy to accept what you say." – "After you've signed our protocol, we shake hands as a sign of our mutual commitment. Remember, a commitment is binding, you can't walk away from it any more.

I confirm your signature and you are a free man to appear with me in front of the magistrate in two weeks' time."

I'm not saying that the legal procedure has been exactly upheld in both cases. Different characters require different approaches also from the law. How could it help an offender to be intimidated or be encouraged repeating his attitude only because being misunderstood.

It's worth the effort to 'twist' rules in order to achieve better outcomes. One and the same rule cannot cover all cases. The word 'twisting' can also be used for other purposes than to legally help little qualified clients in front of the law.

Smart people or the 'sharks' would twist the law with whatever is in their power, not excluding legal professsionals. Where those stakes are high, big money is also playing its role. We solicitors cannot deny it and close our eyes. Only by knowing it, we can control it.

The two proceeding cases were generally speaking in a 'lower' legal category. Not only in an individual appearance of the clients but also how the official legal representation handled their cases.

5.) 'SMART-TWISTERS'

The 'smart-twisters' territory is to bypass the 'old' and 'new' school.

Everything is here more sophisticated and lengthier legal procedures.

An assumed hearing with a solicitor could look like this: The reception has received the client, who has an appointment with the law-firm:

"What a marvellous sunshine we have today! It's a pity for everybody of us to be here. But what can we do? We let the sun shine on my case, too." – The client introduces himself. – "Your personal solicitor is awaiting you, please wait a moment here, I let him know that you have arrived." – "You are one minute early. How are you today? May I ask you to follow me into my office?" – "My pleasure, I hope you too have been all right." – "I can't complain, because if I do, nobody would listen." - "Let's make sure, there is no complaints left after I leave your office". – "You know, we are doing only our best for you." – "How far have you come with my case? You know, performance means, no losers. And that's all I expect not only from me but from people that work for me. Poor performance is not on. I cannot afford it. We are running on a budget. Are we on target?" – "Yes, but also we need to increase our efforts in order to achieve your wanted results within the original time-frame." – "This can wait until you deliver the results. It's your choice, losing the lot or have a sweet win." – "On a positive note I can tell you, the documentation of your case is complete. All what it needs is your signature, so that it can go into the legal battle-fields. I'll lead the court-battle. Our outcome is almost certain as the arguments of the other side haven't been by now convincing. Good contacts are already half the battle at least." – "Here is my signature and I'm off. More important things are awaiting me. Keep working harder for your important client and I will not disappoint you either." – "I'm deeply indebted to you as a valued client. It's my personal pleasure to accompany you back to our reception. Have a pleasant day and I keep you informed.- Are you by the way a rugby-fan? I watch tonight's game.

For which team we should keep our fingers crossed?" – "What a question! The 'Broncos' of course!" – "I knew, we have the same interests! Watch your feet, when you walk down the few steps to the elevator. I better come with you." – "There is no need, I'm all right, thanks!"

Everything is here 'twisted'. Formality only helps to keep confidentiality in files and beyond. As was already mentioned, the level of communication and legal proceedings are more sophisticated, therefore less trans-parent for the outsider. Where money is involved, sophistication comes in. Money is spent more with sophistication than it is earned with sophistication. Money hasn't got much sophistication, but when it comes to spending it, people attach sophistication to money or call it also conditions, because money means power. The more money plays its role, the more power can be attached to it.

"The law-firm I'm working with, is on that side of an 'equation', where money determines the course of proceedings. This is of course not official. It is just self-regulated: people without money don't come through our door. And if somebody comes accidentally to us with not enough convincing background, we point out very politely that he/she must have used the 'wrong door'. Such an internal company-strategy demands maximum attention to operational details, so that the said strategy can work also outside in other related legal establishments like courts. 'The light in our legal tunnel is not visible from the beginning, it can get messy on the way. The main thing is, there is no mess at the end'. My wife Amy and I are sometimes at home in discussions with each other at logger-heads about the differences in our legal work. Amy works hard on her side making the legal system to work and I do the same on my side. It's just different avenues, which in the end lead to the same result: justice is maintained.

One not so insignificant difference is however that my work brings more money. In our life at home together, it doesn't matter. All our earnings go into one and the same pot, so that Amy also benefits from it.

Amy's and my work-days stop at five o'clock in the afternoon. This is traffic-rush-hour again. We usually stay back in the city on a shopping spree, meet friends quite often or have a refreshments in the outdoor cafeterias of the city-mall. A bit later in the afternoon, traffic out of the city starts easing. It's then time to head back home with our car.

At home some work is also waiting. Amy prepares dinner in the kitchen, while I catch up with necessary maintenance around the house.

During the week, we are not keen to go out, because when coming home the dusk has already arrived, depending on the time of the year.

Our leisure-time is on the weekends. It's here and then we catch up with what we like best to do: more shop-ping, see other family-members, play tennis and spend also some time at home. During week-nights, not much time is left for something else than TV and eventually reading.

Occasionally we both have to do some work for the law-firm at home, which is necessary in order to cut back a pile of work from time to time.

There is not much else I can say about Amy's and my life as a solicitor and 'law-twister'.

SOLICITOR / 'LAW-TWISTER' – CONCLUSION

How do legal professionals perform compare with other professions? Barry and Amy had their say. How much are they now 'comedians'? Their position in the society cannot make them immune from the 'comedians'. "Where is sunshine, there is also shade".

The 'comedians' are not out in the 'sun'. By their nature, the 'comedians' are hiding, working the 'brakes', so that nobody gets lost in the 'fast lanes' of life. The law and the money attached to it are the 'comedians' of the legal professionals. They can 'twist' this 'marriage' but not escape from it. More money can lead to detours in legal procedures which in the end must come home to 'mother law'. Money and power are generally known good, strong 'neighbours'. Whoever enters this neighbourhood, finds himself in an 'comedian-territory'.

Legal professionals are also tenants of this 'neighbourhood'. 'Make or 'brake' it', is the house-rule in the 'comedian-world'.

EPILOGUE

"The end justifies the means". And how have here 'means' justified an end? Ten chapters of professions and the establishments have got their say in this first volume. Many more could follow in more volumes. The question is now, how is this number one volume going to perform in the eyes of different readers? If you, the reader, could quietly keep smiling to yourself, neither become overly excited nor felt bored, the author is a happy person, too. The book invites you to look at your mirror-image and if you are true to yourself and other people, you might recognise old and new images in this book not only from yourself, but from many others.

A mixture in style and elements have created something which could be called between a 'comedy' and 'satire'. Not all is a laughing-stock, a comedy stands for, or a mockery of a satire. Initially I've to admit that I was not sure whether to give a preference to a 'comedy' or 'satire'. How about, we call it something new: 'Multicultural Writing'.

Criticism in this book is meant to be constructive. To do away with criticism, is like self-praise with the blinkers on. The end of a road is already reached with knowledge, while questioning keeps us on a road, which we like to see leading towards real progress.

If a reader for instance 'knows everything', then is no point for him/her to read any more.

I, the author, have remained on a road of observation, listened to other people and still do. This all has given a spark to my writing, too.

"There is always more than the eye can see". "Beggars & other Comedians" is exactly this 'more' what the eye can only eventually see.

www.ingramcontent.com/pod-product-compliance
Lightning Source LLC
Chambersburg PA
CBHW030549080526
44585CB00012B/314